ALFARABI

*Philosophy of
Plato and Aristotle*

AGORA EDITIONS

Editor: Thomas L. Pangle

Founding Editor: Allan Bloom

Alfarabi, *Philosophy of Plato and Aristotle*. Translated by Muhsin Mahdi.

Alfarabi, *The Political Writings: "Selected Aphorisms" and Other Texts*. Translated by Charles E. Butterworth

Bolotin, David. *Plato's Dialogue on Friendship: An Interpretation of the "Lysis," with a New Translation.*

Kojève, Alexandre. *Introduction to the Reading of Hegel: Lectures on the "Phenomenology of Spirit."* Assembled by Raymond Queneau. Edited by Allan Bloom. Translated by James H. Nichols Jr.

Medieval Political Philosophy: A Sourcebook. Edited by Ralph Lerner and Muhsin Mahdi.

Plato. *Gorgias.* Translated by James H. Nichols Jr.

Plato. *Phaedrus.* Translated by James H. Nichols Jr.

Plato. *Gorgias and Phaedrus.* Translated by James H. Nichols Jr.

The Roots of Political Philosophy: Ten Forgotten Socratic Dialogues. Edited by Thomas L. Pangle.

Rousseau, Jean-Jacques. *Politics and the Arts: Letter to M. D'Alembert on the Theatre.* Translated by Allan Bloom.

Xenophon. *The Education of Cyrus.* Translated by Wayne Ambler.

Xenophon. *Memorabilia.* Translated by Amy L. Bonnette.

ALFARABI
Philosophy of
Plato and Aristotle

TRANSLATED, WITH AN INTRODUCTION

BY MUHSIN MAHDI

REVISED EDITION

with a Foreword by
Charles E. Butterworth
and Thomas L. Pangle

Cornell University Press
ITHACA, NEW YORK

First published 1962 by the Free Press of Glencoe
Revised ed., first published 1969 by Cornell University Press
First printing of revised ed., Cornell Paperbacks, 1969
First printing with new foreword, Cornell Paperbacks, 2001

Printed in the United States of America

Library of Congress Cataloging-in-Publication Data

Farabi.
    [Selections. English. 2001]
    Alfarabi's philosophy of Plato and Aristotle / translated, with an
introduction, by Muhsin Mahdi.—Rev. ed.
        p. cm. — (Agora editions)
    Originally published: 1969. With new foreword.
    Includes bibliographical references and index.
    ISBN-13: 978-0-8014-8716-3 (pbk. : alk. paper)
    ISBN-10: 0-8014-8716-1 (pbk. : alk. paper)
    1. Happiness. 2. Plato—Contributions in concept of happiness. 3.
Aristotle—Contributions in concept of happiness. 4. Philosophy,
Ancient. I. Title: Philosophy of Plato and Aristotle. II. Mahdi,
Muhsin. III. Title. IV. Agora Editions (Cornell University Press)
    B753.F33 .A25 2001
    181'.6—dc21   2001047329

Cornell University Press strives to use environmentally responsible
suppliers and materials to the fullest extent possible in the publishing
of its books. Such materials include vegetable-based, low-VOC inks
and acid-free papers that are recycled, totally chlorine-free, or partly
composed of nonwood fibers. For further information, visit our website
at www.cornellpress.cornell.edu.

Paperback printing   10 9 8 7 6 5 4 3

CONTENTS

PREFACE

The opportunity provided by this paperback edition has been used to add a new Introduction, with the hope of aiding the reader in reflecting on the account of the theoretical sciences in the *Attainment of Happiness*. I have also been able to correct some mistakes in the text and the notes, to make a few stylistic changes, and to reconsider a few of the interpolations.

Since the first publication of the book in 1962, I have had access to a sizable body of additional manuscript material relating to the Arabic text in various libraries in Iran and Turkey. It includes a number of previously unknown manuscript copies of the *Attainment of Happiness*, a number of extracts from the *Attainment of Happiness* and the *Philosophy of Aristotle*, and an extensive paraphrase of the *Philosophy of Plato* and the *Philosophy of Aristotle*, by ʿAbd al-Laṭīf al-Baghdādī (1162–1231) preserved in Bursa (Hüseyin Çelebi, No. 823, fols. 79v–87v). While helpful in clarifying a few places in the text (see Part III, sec. 99, n. 9), none of it appears to correspond to the fuller version used by Falaquera for his Hebrew paraphrase (see p. 152). Nevertheless, I hope to be able to examine it more closely when the opportunity for a new edition of the Arabic text of the trilogy presents itself.

Muhsin Mahdi

Chicago, 1968

vi «

FOREWORD

Charles E. Butterworth and Thomas L. Pangle

About eleven centuries ago, when any memory of the true meaning of classical political philosophy was on the verge of disappearing from the earth, Alfarabi (Abū Naṣr Muḥammad ibn Muḥammad ibn Ṭarkhān ibn Awzalagh al-Fārābī, ca. 870–950) launched from within the world of Islam an extraordinary project of resuscitation. Alfarabi was guided, he indicates, by what he understood to be Plato's and Aristotle's instructions as to "the ways to re-establish" true philosophy "when it becomes confused or extinct."[1] Through his commentaries, logical treatises, and above all his writings in political philosophy, Alfarabi succeeded to an extraordinary degree, becoming known as "the second teacher"—second, that is, after Aristotle. He spawned a great tradition of Aristotelian/Platonic political philosophy in the medieval world of Islamic and Arabic culture, a tradition whose brightest stars are Avicenna (980–1037), Ibn Ṭufayl (ca. 1110–1185), Averroes (1126–98), and Maimonides (1135–1204).[2] Through these great intermediaries, Alfarabi's impulse became a leading inspiration of medieval Aristotelianism in the Christian world.

Yet this success incurred, over time, severe costs. On the political and religious level, there arose a reaction within Islam, spearheaded intellectually by the theologian and sometime jurist Alghazali (1058–1111) that eventually culminated in the successful persecution and eradication of philosophy.[3] On the philosophic level, the transmission of the original Alfarabian impulse, especially to and through Christianity, involved a transmogrification and obfuscation of Alfarabi's own understanding of the nature of "true philosophy." There came to be established a basic scholarly and philosophic consensus, which prevails to this day, regarding the rhetorical character, the substance, and the validity of Platonic and Aristotelian writing: a consensus that is dramatically opposed to and by Alfarabi's understanding. Until the rediscovery of the authentic teachings and arguments of Alfarabi by Leo Strauss,[4] all knowledge of Alfarabi's radically alien and provocatively challenging conception of Platonic-Aristotelian political philosophy as the key to the final truth about the human condition had been lost. For it is Alfarabi's contention that "*the true* philosophy," according to which "the idea of Imam, Philosopher, and Legislator is a single idea," was "handed down to us by the Greeks from Plato and Aristotle *only*." "Let it be clear to you that, in what they presented, their purpose is the same, and that they intended to offer *one* and the *same* philosophy" (*AH* sec. 57, 42:12–13 and sects. 63–64, 47: 3 ff.; emphases added).

This book and its successors make available to modern students the texts in which Alfarabi advances and defends his astounding philosophic and interpretative claims. In these writings are to be found the searing Alfarabian doubts about all present-day "canonical" readings of Plato and Aristotle as well as all "canonical" conceptions of the true meaning, aim, and truth of classical political philosophy.

The key to Alfarabi's project is his historical context—or, more precisely, that one massive aspect of his historical situation to which Alfarabi himself repeatedly draws attention. Alfarabi came to Platonic philosophy in a world dominated by the Quran, together with the Hebrew and Christian Bible.[5] Every authority, Christian and Jewish as well as Islamic, dinned into Alfarabi and his young peers the claim that the writings of Plato and Aristotle, given their ignorance of the Holy Scriptures and of the God there revealed, could not possibly have answered the challenge that religious faith at its fullest or truest poses to all claims of unassisted, merely human, all-too-human, reason. The classical philosophers could be considered extremely helpful supplements or even alternatives to Scripture. But these "ancients" could not have anticipated, and therefore could not have provided adequate resources for a response to, scriptural revelation. What is more, fundamental to Islam as to Judaism was a divine law set forth by a divinely sanctioned prophet; before these, philosophic law-giving had to be defended.

Such a fundamental questioning of classical rationalism is not peculiar to Alfarabi's epoch. This apparently conclusive restriction of classical rationalism has continued to our own time, and now represents the single most decisive objection to any attempt to return to classical philosophy as the source of comprehensive truth about the human condition. Yet one can and must go further. This apparently overwhelming difficulty caused the construction of the alternative—namely, distinctively modern—rationalism, the "Enlightenment." With the collapse of modern rationalism, a collapse that has brought in its train our reigning historical and cultural relativism, it looks as though this apparent restriction on classical rationalism is the deepest reason for what we are experiencing as the death of rationalism. To state the same matter differently, this apparently overwhelming difficulty is the compelling ground for the triumph of Heideggerian postmodernism and its denial of the possibility to grasp permanent, universally objective, moral and epistemological standards by means of reason.

To this crisis of rationalism which grips our planetary culture, Alfarabi speaks—with an intransigence unrivaled in the history of philosophy. For Alfarabi made it his chief purpose to indicate how the theological-political thought of Plato fully anticipated and completely accounted for the core of the new challenge offered by scriptural revelations. Alfarabi sets out to show the attentive reader that political philosophy (what he terms "political science" or "practical science") as conceived by Plato and Aristotle—and thus as expressed in a life of ceaseless questioning of others and of oneself through "dialectical conversation"—succeeds in laying the conceptual foundation for any authentically empirical and deductive natural science, as well as for an understanding of civic and intellectual virtue experienced as "the attainment of happiness." (Note that it is the *attainment*, not merely the *pursuit*, of happiness!)

Such a summary of Alfarabi's ultimate and radically anti-authoritarian aim suffices to show why he so emphatically declares that "the perfect human, the human who investigates, and the virtuous human are in grave danger."[6] Alfarabi clearly recognizes that society cannot tolerate the full and open expression of the attainment of happiness. It therefore becomes necessary for the true philosopher to engage in a meticulously artful self-hiding and philanthropic rhe-

torical manipulation. In one of his most startling interpretative sug-
gestions, Alfarabi insists the chief teaching of Plato's *Republic* is
that the true philosopher must go beyond "the method of Socrates"
in order to embrace and to perfect "the method of Thrasymachus"—which is "more able to form the character of the youth
and instruct the multitude."[7] And Alfarabi makes it abundantly clear
that he himself practices what he understands Plato to teach about
the defective and hence extraordinarily delicate nature of all public
and especially written communication (*PP* secs. 27–28, 16:1–10).

The reader needs, then, to become familiar with Alfarabi's
highly original, extremely difficult, but ultimately very beautiful
reenactment of the Platonic art of sophistic writing. That art is
calculated to prevent the abuse of philosophic truth by most (who
are casual readers) as it teaches a few (who are willing to work
and to learn) how to think, how to observe with the detective's eye
of one who goes through life in the greatest possible state of al-
ertness and openness and self-protective caution. With a view to
highlighting Alfarabi's use of this Platonic art, a few of his most
pervasive literary devices deserve some brief explanation.

First and most amazing is Alfarabi's Platonic penchant for stat-
ing more or less boldly some of his paradoxical *conclusions* while
leaving it to the reader to piece together, and in part to discover
(to reenact and thus truly to drink in), the experiential reasoning
that makes the conclusions cogent. (A relatively easy example of
this device is Alfarabi's declaration that "philosophy is prior to
religion in time," *AH* sec. 55, 41:12.) Alfarabi thus succeeds in
allowing most readers to brush off as preposterous some existential
truths whose utterance will provoke a few "anarchists of the spirit"
to rush with anxious delight to the work of discovering how and
why they must reorient their lives. Alfarabi has spoken openly of
this device in perhaps his most charming passage, the parable of
the drunken mystic at the beginning of his *Summary of Plato's
"Laws"*:

> a certain abstemious ascetic was known for his probity, propriety, as-
> ceticism, and worship, and having become famous for this, he feared the
> tyrannical sovereign and wanted to run away from his city. The sover-
> eign's command went out to search for and arrest him wherever he was

found. He could not leave from any of the city's gates and was apprehensive lest he fall into the hands of the sovereign's men. So he went and found a dress worn by vagabonds, put it on, carried a cymbal in his hand, and, pretending to be drunk, came early at night out to the gate of the city singing to the accompaniment of that cymbal of his. The gatekeeper said to him, "Who are you?" "I am so-and-so, the ascetic!" he said jokingly. The gatekeeper supposed he was poking fun at him and did not interfere with him. So he saved himself without having lied in what he said.

Our purpose in making this introduction is this: the wise Plato did not feel free to reveal and uncover every kind of knowledge for all people. Therefore he followed the practice of using symbols, riddles, obscurity, and difficulty, so that knowledge would not fall into the hands of those who do not deserve it and be deformed, or into the hands of someone who does not know its worth or who uses it improperly. In this he was right.

This parable points us more clearly than any other to a second pervasive Alfarabian-Platonic literary device or manner: Alfarabi's ubiquitous archness, his dead-pan ironic wit. Thus, for example, throughout most of the *Attainment of Happiness* and, to a lesser extent, the *Philosophy of Plato*, Alfarabi engages in the charade of speaking as if it were the serious purpose of political philosophy to rule directly over a (new) political order. Only at the end of each work (*AH* sec. 62, 46:12–47:2; *PP* sec. 38, 22:14–23:7) does he suddenly indicate, in elliptical fashion, that this has been a grotesque exaggeration. He has intended to arouse the shocked wonder and hence thought of a few readers while allowing most to believe, in self-congratulatory fashion, in political philosophy as a wildly impractical castle-building-in-Spain.

There is in the third place Alfarabi's brazen[8] commission of self-contradiction—between works, between passages, and even, at least once (*PP* sec. 22, 13:6–11), within the same sentence. The uses of this device are manifold. Alfarabi enables himself simultaneously to embrace and to deny what is "respectable"; or he can make himself appear to "change his mind" back and forth; or he can take the sting out of the shocking by denying it, before or after having affirmed it. More important are the contradictions between statements *neither* of which is altogether respectable: in these cases, the reader is tempted to complacency, to regard Alfarabi as confused and thus as rather harmless in his irritating but obviously scatter-brained thinking. The demanding reader is compelled, however, to figure out which is Alfarabi's true opinion and why the opinion that is not true can nonetheless seem true—thereby illuminating the context which makes it appear true. Let us take the gravest example.

Having opened the *Attainment of Happiness* with the declaration that this attainment requires the theoretical virtues consisting in the sciences which "make the beings and what they contain intelligible with certainty," Alfarabi first presents the order of the sciences as ascending from logic to the quasi-Aristotelian (and thus pagan) science of metaphysics—immediately following the science of physics or of material bodies (*AH* secs. 16–19, 12:14–15:15). In the sequel, the *Philosophy of Plato*, Alfarabi is totally silent about any metaphysical component in his presentation of the "philosophy of Plato . . . from the beginning to the end" (Alfarabi never mentions the ideas). At the end of the *Philosophy of Aristotle*, or the tripartite work as a whole, Alfarabi declares "we do not possess metaphysical science" (sec. 99, 133:1).[9] Having received this stunning news, one of course is impelled to start again, from the beginning. Then one is in a position to take proper note of the fact that the original and apparently very confident proclamation about the importance of the science of metaphysics was followed, in ascending order, by a discussion of the importance of the science of biology. This latter "inquiry," Alfarabi suddenly declares, "will lead one to the same conclusion as" the preceding (i.e., the lower) metaphysical "inquiry." For biology culminates in the science of "the rational animal," and "this investigation will *force* one to look for principles that are not bodies or in bodies, and that never were or ever will be in bodies"—"another genus of things, different from the metaphysical." These are the things "by which he achieves that perfection that became known in natural science." "It will become evident concomitantly that these rational principles are not mere *causes* by which man attains the perfection." On the other hand, one "will know that these rational principles also *supply* many things to natural beings *other* than those supplied by nature."[10] All this helps us when we try to understand the bewildering close of the *Philosophy of Aristotle*: for there, Alfarabi had stated that "our defective natural science, for we do not possess metaphysical science," could be made "perfect" once one understood, as a direct consequence of studying Aristotle's work entitled *Metaphysics*, that "the understanding of the causes of the visible things, which the soul desired, is more human than that knowledge that was construed to be the necessary knowledge."

In this example we note also the device of progressively deepening, in part by thought-provoking contradiction, in part by "repeating" the articulation of a radical thesis (in Alfarabi, as in his master Plato, repetitions never prove to be simply repetitions when closely scrutinized).

Alfarabi's total silence about the ideas vividly illustrates another frequently employed device: pregnant silence. The significance of such silences the reader is always compelled to think through on his own.

Let us not be bashful about underlining the obvious: Alfarabi continually directs his reader to, and expects his reader to have always "at his elbow," the texts of Plato and Aristotle. Given this expectation, Alfarabi can permit himself to say the darnedest things about what one is supposed to be able to find in a particular dialogue or writing. In other words, Alfarabi is not engaged here in writing an interpretative study or commentary; instead he is intent upon restating in a new, playful, and hence arresting way what he has found to be the core of Platonic teaching and argument. (In this he may be said to foreshadow Thomas More's *Utopia*.) Alfarabi forces one to go back and forth between what one thinks one knows of Plato and what one is astonished to see Alfarabi thinks—or does he? To be sure, one learns to read Alfarabi with the awareness that one is playing a game of philosophic poker with a benevolent master teacher, who keeps hinting that you could win possession of your own soul for the first time.

Last but not least, let us note that, as a good teacher, Alfarabi has imposed some very severe entrance examinations. Most obvious is the apparently soporific opening of the *Attainment of Happiness*, which seems almost a mockery of the inviting title. As already noted, the guileful radicalism hidden in the list of sciences begins to appear only when one appreciates yet another Alfarabian device: the relentless refusal to explain the ordering and the transitions within a writing. Only when the reader constantly asks, and makes progress in answering on his own, the question of the reasons for the unfolding order of exposition does the true signal begin to be received.

We have stressed the necessity of moving back and forth from the texts of Alfarabi to the texts of Plato and Aristotle. In no regard is this more important than in respect to Alfarabi's treatment of "dialectic." Dialectic is the art of friendly refutative conversation by which the Platonic Socrates "converts" a select few of the young. He takes them from an adherence to the world as conceived by prephilosophic life (the "cave") to a radically different, because simply true or enlightened, experience of the world. Alfarabi never depicts this activity. He proceeds as if no one who has access to Plato's texts needs further or better depictions. What Alfarabi does contribute is crucial instruction in what Plato leaves much more obscure (and what Alfarabi evidently thought had been utterly lost sight of in his time): the precise character of the foundational scientific significance of this "dialectical" activity or of its empirically evident aftermath. We close this foreword by introducing this most important theme.

The *Philosophy of Plato* playfully elaborates the entire Platonic enterprise as a sequential quest. In truth, this quest is not meant by Alfarabi to be a historical account of what happened to Plato. It is instead an archetypal account of the stages in a truly philosophic life, of which the Alfarabian "Plato" is the paradigm. The *first* stage of the quest culminates when it "became evident" to Plato that "the attainment of happiness" consists in "the knowledge of the substance of each of the beings"; and that the good "state of character" and "virtuous way of life" is what leads to the acquisition of such knowledge (*PP* secs. 2–4, 3:12–4:10). This beginning point exemplifies one of the leading characteristics of Alfarabi: we believe it is fair to say that no writer before or since him has ever so intransigently contended that the theoretical way of life was the one and the only true fulfillment of human existence. But this point also raises an obvious question: why, if "Plato" at the *start* already has an answer to the question of the attainment of happiness or the fulfillment of humanity, does he need to continue his quest? Why does he not simply proceed to a scientific study of the nature of things?

The answer—or the fundamental question that propels "Plato" on his quest—is immediately given by Alfarabi, as he turns to the crucial second stage (PP sec. 5, 4:13ff.). "Plato" comes face to face with the challenge of radical, Protagorean relativism. "If a human being should aspire to a knowledge of the being that has this character, *can he attain it?* Or is it the case—as Protagoras ... asserts—that humanity cannot attain such knowledge of the beings, that ... the knowledge natural to man is relative to the conviction formed by each individual ...?"

Now Alfarabi proceeds to report that "Plato explained that, contrary to what Protagoras asserts, this knowledge can be attained and does exist." But this of course leaves us wondering, how is this demonstrated? And why is "Plato" necessarily so arrested by this challenge? What is behind this challenge that makes it so troubling, and why is "Plato" compelled to set aside the obvious course of his progress, and find his way along an entirely new philosophic detour, in order to deal with this challenge? These are the questions that guide the rest of the book.

The next step (*PP* sec. 6, 5:9–6:2), and the first massive hint, is a confrontation with the claim that while such knowledge exists, it is available not by any human effort but only by what "Plato" came to regard as "nature and chance." Alfarabi assures us that "Plato" disposes also of this claim—but Alfarabi does not explain how. Again, he leaves us to puzzle over why this is the massive alternative that necessarily presents itself immediately after the encounter with Protagoras (see sec. 5, 4:11–5:8), thereby illuminating the significance of that encounter.

Alfarabi does offer great help in dispelling our puzzlement when he proceeds to the next step (*PP* sec. 7, 6:3–17, esp. 10–17). Granted that the fundamental knowledge is acquired by human effort, "Plato" must immediately investigate whether it is "religious speculation" and "religious investigation of the beings" (what we would call "theology") that "supply this knowledge and that desired way of life." The outcome of this investigation—carried out, Alfarabi says, in the *Euthyphro*—is disconcertingly inconclusive. To "Plato" only this much "becomes clear": that "religious" thinking "is not sufficient."

This is the beginning of a similarly inconclusive series of investigations into the kinds of knowledge provided by (in apparently ascending order) linguistics, poetry, rhetoric, and sophistry (*PP* secs. 8–11, 7:1–9:2). We can easily become increasingly disappointed as we watch Plato's quest unfold, until (*PP* sec. 12, 9:3–10) he turns to an "inquiry into the investigations of the dialecticians and into the dialectical investigation." For Plato

> explained that it is extremely valuable for arriving at that knowledge; indeed, frequently it is impossible to come to that knowledge until the thing is investigated dialectically. It does not supply that knowledge from the outset, however. No, in order to attain that knowledge, another faculty is needed along with, and in addition to, the faculty for dialectical exercise.

Our poker-faced teacher refuses, however, to say another word about what that faculty is.

But his tantalizing silence hones our minds to appreciate the significance of what he says later, in his most important sentence on "the method of Socrates" (*PP* sec. 36, 22:4–5). There we find that Plato "explained" that Socrates possessed "only the ability to conduct a scientific investigation of justice and the virtues, *and a power [faculty] of love*" (emphasis added). For, as "Plato explained" previously (*PP* sec. 25, 14:4–15:17), the result of his investigation into "how the man who is resolved to become a philosopher or a statesman and achieve something good ought to be" was to find that "rapture," or a certain "reveling," must "continue to be in him" so long as he still "seeks the virtuous end." Or as Alfarabi said in his own name, in the preliminary *Attainment of Happiness* (sec. 60, 44:13–45:11), "he who sets out to inquire" not only should possess rare theoretical gifts but "should *love*" both "justice and just people" while being "high-minded" and "pious"; "he should have sound conviction about the opinion of the religion in which he is reared, hold fast to the virtuous acts in his religion, and not forsake all or most of them." "For if a youth is such, and *then* sets out to study philosophy," then "it is *possible* that he will not become a counterfeit or a vain or a false philosopher" (emphases added).

To pick up again the thread of the account of "Plato's" quest, immediately after the laudatory discussion of dialectic, Alfarabi repeats himself—or rather, speaks as though what he has just said about dialectic had not been said. He declares (*PP* sec. 13, 9:11–10:6) that when Plato "had exhausted all the generally accepted scientific or theoretical arts and found that none of them supplies this knowledge of the beings or that way of life, he began next to investigate the practical. . . ." The turn to "dialectic" and the turn to "the practical" are identical. In other words, Alfarabi reports that dialectic begins when "Plato" engages in the characteristic Socratic turn to the lowly arts and crafts, in which is discovered the clearest employment of human reason in action—seeking, Alfarabi stresses, nothing but some "utility" or "gain." But (Alfarabi adds) the outcome of this investigation is that "the useful may be necessary, while the gainful is always virtuous."[11] This unexpected discovery provokes unusual wonder: for, Alfarabi says, when this result "had come to light," he "began to investigate what the necessary is and what the gainful is" (sec. 14, 10:7–15). And then Alfarabi uncharacteristically interjects himself, so as to skip suddenly to the outcome of all this, inditing what may well be the single most important sentence in the entire work:

> there is no difference between investigating gain, what is gainful, and what is virtuous/noble, for these are almost synonyms referring to the same idea.

(This is what the best living expositor of Plato has called "the fundamental fact."[12] It was limned most nobly by Plato when he stressed in the *Republic* [526e] that "the idea of the good," which "our soul discerns" when "it is compelled to turn to the place where resides the happiest part of existence," ranks far above and must be understood as the standard and even the source of the ideas of the just, the pious, and the noble.) Alfarabi reports that the subsequent investigation of what is truly gainful culminates in the investigation into the "pleasure-seekers' way of life" (*PP* sec. 18, 12:1–6). The conclusion is: "no part of the pleasure-seekers' way of life leads to the pleasure originating in the desired perfection. This is to be found in his ["Plato's"] book *On Pleasure*, which is attributed to Socrates." Thus does Alfarabi finally name Socrates for the first time.

Immediately thereafter, Alfarabi reports that "Plato" is *now* finally in a position to explain "what the idea of the philosopher is and what his activity is" (*PP* sec. 19, 12:15–16). This activity includes most prominently the investigation of the "practical" or "political" art and the virtues of moderation, courage, love, and friendship—culminating in "that which is true friendship and love" (*PP* secs. 21–24, 13:3–14:3). But Alfarabi insists that Plato insists that "philosophy" is first and foremost "the theoretical art that supplies the knowledge of the beings" (*PP* sec. 19, 12:11). Still, "he explained in his book known as the *Erastai* that philosophy is not merely a virtuous thing; no, it is that which is truly useful" (*PP* sec. 20, 13:1–2). Accordingly, the remainder of the Platonic quest as reported by Alfarabi concerns chiefly how one ought to understand and live the proper relationship between the philosopher and the nonphilosophers (*PP* secs. 29–38, 16:11–23:8). For, as Alfarabi stresses in his own name in the *Attainment of Happiness* (sec. 54, 39:9–10), "when the theoretical sciences are isolated and their possessor does not have the faculty for exploiting them for the benefit of others, they are defective philosophy."

NOTES

1. *Attainment of Happiness* (henceforth *AH*; references are to the sections of the translated text as well as to the pages and lines of the Hyderabad edition of the Arabic, as indicated in the margins of the present volume) sec. 63, 47:6.

2. In whose exacting judgment, "all of his [Alfarabi's] writings are faultlessly excellent"; see letter to Samuel Ibn Tibbon, quoted by Shlomo Pines, "Translator's Introduction," in *The Guide of the Perplexed* (Chicago, 1963), lix–lx. From this important letter it would appear that while Maimonides regarded Aristotle as "the extreme of human intellect," he had an even higher regard for Alfarabi's writings than for those of either Plato or Aristotle. A chief reason for such an appreciation will become evident in a moment.

3. The most readable account of the extinction of the philosophic tradition founded by Alfarabi is still Ernest Renan's *Averroès et l'Averroïsme, Essai historique*, in *Oeuvres complètes de Ernest Renan*, vol. 3 (Paris, 1949); for Alghazali's most important work against philosophy, see *The Incoherence of the Philosophers*, ed. and trans. Michael Marmura (Provo, Utah, 1997).

4. See especially "Farabi's Plato," in *Louis Ginzburg Jubilee Volume* (New York, 1945); reprinted in Arthur Hyman, ed., *Essays in Medieval Jewish and Islamic Philosophy* (New York, 1977).

5. Alfarabi studied in Baghdad under the Nestorian Christian Aristotelians Yūḥannā Ibn Ḥaylān and Abū Bishr Mattā ibn Yūnus—the latter a great Greek scholar and translator. Apparently, literal Arabic translations of at least Plato's *Laws, Republic,* and *Timaeus* were available to Alfarabi; it is not known how he gained access to the other dialogues he discusses. Remarkable projects of literal translations of Greek philosophic works into Arabic and Syriac had been undertaken in the two generations prior to Alfarabi's birth. Especially noteworthy is the translation project patronized by the Abbasid ruler al-Ma'mūn, who reigned 813–833, and his successors; the best known of his Greek scholar-translators were Ḥunayn ibn Isḥāq, 809–873, and his son Isḥāq (d. 911). In the city of Ḥarrān, where Alfarabi studied, was a major translation center led by Thābit ibn Qurra (ca. 836–901).

6. *Philosophy of Plato* (henceforth *PP*; references are to the sections of the translated text as well as to the pages and lines of the Rosenthal and Walzer edition of the Arabic, as indicated in the margins of the present volume) sec. 38, 22:14–18.

7. *PP* sec. 36, 21:15–22:8. See also sec. 11, 8:7–9:2. Note that the attack on "hypocrites," such as Hippias, at sec. 17, 11:4–15, is explicitly not an attack on true "sophistry," the "value" of which Plato "explained"—that is, all true sophists are liars, but not all liars or even apparent sophists are true sophists. The textual basis in the *Republic* vindicating Alfarabi's insight is found especially at 498c–d, in the light of 492d–e and above all 493d5, which implies that there is a "necessary" employment of sophistry by the virtuous man.

8. This device is particularly shameless given Alfarabi's fully justified reputation as having authored some of the best philosophic treatises ever written on logic and on the nature of false reasoning or contradiction (see again, in this regard, Maimonides' letter to Ibn Tibbon: "as for works on logic, one should *only* study the writings of Abū Naṣr al-Fārābī"; emphasis added).

9. References to the *Philosophy of Aristotle,* henceforth *PA,* are to the sections of the translated text as well as to the pages and lines of the Beirut edition of the Arabic, as indicated in the margins of the present volume.

10. *AH* secs. 17–18, 13:1–14:2. The next item, ascending from the science of man as the culmination of biology, is, again, to our surprise, metaphysics— which now culminates in the knowledge that "the first principle is the divinity" (secs. 18–19, 14:2–15:15). Yet this is not, contrary to expectation, the peak of theoretical science. That peak is occupied (or wrested away) by "political science," whose focus is "the good, virtuous, and noble things." In political science, these things are initially approached or *"investigated"* as the things "by which man achieves" the "purpose for which man is made," i.e., "the perfection that man must achieve"; but the *result* of the investigation is an absolutely certain *"knowledge"* that these are in fact "things by which the citizens of cities attain *happiness"*—nay (Alfarabi repeats himself), *"supreme* happiness" (the prominent reference in the first sentence of the whole work to the "supreme happiness in the next life" is totally purged after political science, and the successful

conclusion of its specific investigation, has been brought on stage). See secs. 20–21, 15:16–16:18; also *PA* sec. 3, 62:14–23, on the source of "certainty" in practical science, this certainty being "the perfect science of what one wants to know and the end beyond which one can hope for no better assurance and reliability." Compare David Bolotin, *An Approach to Aristotle's Physics: With Particular Attention to the Role of His Manner of Writing* (Albany, 1998), 154 n. 12.

11. As Mahdi indicates in a footnote, the Arabic here and in what follows is *fāḍil*; the Greek equivalent would be *kalon*.

12. Christopher Bruell, "On Plato's Political Philosophy," *Review of Politics* 56:2 (1994), 265.

INTRODUCTION TO THE

REVISED EDITION

The stated aim of the *Attainment of Happiness* is to describe true philosophy and distinguish it from counterfeit, vain, and false philosophy. Alfarabi and his contemporaries possessed two accounts of this true philosophy together with the ways to it and the ways to reconstruct it when it becomes confused or extinct (Part I, sec. 63). In the *Philosophy of Plato* and the *Philosophy of Aristotle,* Alfarabi expounds these two accounts so the reader can comprehend their unity of purpose and intention. The *Attainment of Happiness* is a reconstruction of the philosophy of Plato and Aristotle which seeks to remove the confusion about the purpose and intention of that philosophy.

The principal theme of the *Attainment of Happiness* concerns human things—the levels of human happiness and the human attainments (the theoretical virtues, calculative or deliberative virtues, moral virtues, and practical arts) by which happiness is achieved by citizens of nations and cities. In principle, all men in all nations and all cities are assumed to be capable of pursuing happiness by making use of and perfecting the things that constitute their particular nature and excellence as human beings and distinguish them from other natural beings and from divine beings. These distinctively human things are the virtues and arts whose development requires the exercise of will and choice, and are not merely the product of nature, or chance, or some other extraneous cause.

In making happiness the dominant theme of his book, Alfarabi departs from his Aristotle, who is silent about happiness. And in making it the initial theme of his book, he departs from his Plato as well. His Plato and Aristotle begin by investigating the perfection of man as man. This investigation leads to the human virtues and arts through which man realizes his perfection and to the human association—the city—in which it is realized. Alfarabi reverses this procedure. Assuming, as it were, the results of the investigations of Plato and Aristotle, he begins by enumerating the four kinds of human things by which citizens of nations and cities attain every level of happiness, and then proceeds to investigate them. In substituting happiness for perfection, in beginning with citizens of nations and cities rather than with man as man, and in starting by declaring his intention to deal with the question of the attainment or realization of happiness and the things that produce it, Alfarabi appears more practical or political, not only when compared with his Aristotle, but even when compared with his Plato.

Human things in general, and happiness in particular, are thought to be the subject, not of science as a whole, but of practical and political science. Following the lead given by Alfarabi in the fifth chapter of the *Enumeration of the Sciences,* Averroes suggests at the beginning of his *Paraphrase of Plato's Republic* that the *Attainment of Happiness* deals with the first or theoretical part of political science, the part which investigates the general rules that are further away from action, as distinguished from the second part, which investigates the less general rules that are nearer to action. Averroes states that the first part of political science is contained in Aristotle's *Ethics,* while the second part is contained in Aristotle's *Politics* and in Plato's *Republic.* Accordingly, the *Attainment of Happiness* should correspond to Aristotle's *Ethics* rather than to Plato's *Republic.* This view is based on the classification of the sciences suggested in the *Ethics.* Yet the unity of the purpose and intention of Plato and Aristotle in political science, to which Alfarabi points by bringing together the *Ethics* and the *Republic,* does not leave room for this classification. Alfarabi avoids and appears to reject the distinction between theoretical and practical science, theoretical and practical reason, and the premises or principles of theoretical and practical reason, which is the basis of the Aristotelian view of politics as a practical science (cf. Alfarabi, *Statesman,* secs. 35, 42). His intention to disregard the Aristotelian classification of the sciences in the *Ethics* is implied in his opening statement, which incorporates the theoretical virtues within a human or political framework. Even the expression "practical virtue" does not appear until after Alfarabi concludes the investigation of the human virtues and arts and determines their contribution to man's highest perfection (I, secs. 41 ff.).

All of Aristotle's theoretical sciences are included in the discussion of the theoretical virtues, which consist of "the sciences whose ultimate purpose is only to make the beings and what they contain intelligible with certainty" (I, sec. 2). So also are the characteristic features of Aristotle's logic. Incorporation of the results of Aristotle's investigations is evident in the distinction between primary and acquired knowledge; in the systematic inquiry into the kinds of premises, arguments, and conclusions, prior to, or separate from, the investigation of the beings and their attributes; in the distinction between the principles of instruction and the principles of being and the classification of the causes of beings and classes of proofs; and in the progressive movement toward causes from their effects and back from causes to their effects, until the mind discovers the structure of the beings and their articulation into species and genera (I, sec. 2–9). The extended treatment of these methodological questions is justified by the frequency with which "we" fail to attain certainty and attain some kind of "belief"—because we lack the science that enables us to distinguish the various methods—and by the prevalence of this uncertainty among "the great majority of the speculators and investigators we see around us" (I, sec. 3; cf. I, sec. 60; see Averroes, *Commentary on the Metaphysics*, p. 1397; Maimonides, *Eight Chapters*, ch. 4, p. 18:2–3, Wolff, ed.). Furthermore, when distinguishing the various methods (I, sec. 4), Alfarabi lists what corresponds to demonstrative, sophistical, rhetorical, and poetic reasoning, in this order, but omits dialectical reasoning. The tendency to deprecate dialectic is one of the hallmarks of Alfarabi's Aristotle. (Cf. III, sec. 3, end, 15–16, and the subordination of dialectic to demonstration in III, sec. 13, par. 1: the order in which Alfarabi enumerates the remaining four kinds of reasoning corresponds to the order in which his Aristotle investigates them in III, secs. 7–16, provided one omits dialectic altogether.) He follows the lead of his Aristotle also in omitting the methods pursued in religious and linguistic investigations, with which his Plato began canvassing the generally accepted arts (II, secs. 7–8; cf. Alfarabi, *Enumeration of the Sciences,* chs. 1, 5). The remaining four arts investigated by his Plato are poetry, rhetoric, sophistry, and dialectic, in this order. Alfarabi, then, substitutes his Aristotle's art of demonstration for his Plato's dialectic, and follows his Aristotle's lead in reversing the order in which his Plato investigated these arts. The reversal of his Plato's procedure assumes that the quest for the certain science has reached its goal. The theoretical sciences can now be investigated, and theoretical perfection attained, prior to the investigation of the other and lower methods and arts. These are no longer seen as necessary steps on the way to the discovery of the highest art but as methods that assume the existence of demonstrative science and merely serve it and help to protect it.

The account of the activity of the theoretical virtues or theoretical sciences, which is placed by Alfarabi at the beginning of the *Attainment of Happiness,* concludes with the assertion that theoretical perfection comprises knowledge of the four kinds of things by which citizens attain supreme happiness (I, sec. 21)—that is, the theoretical virtues, the deliberative virtues, the moral virtues, and the practical arts. What begins as a thoroughly Aristotelian account of the theoretical sciences concludes by departing from Aristotle's somewhat sharp distinction between the theoretical and practical sciences in that it includes as part of theoretical perfection things that, according to Aristotle, belong to practical rather than to theoretical science. For Alfarabi's theoretical perfection appears to include all the Aristotelian theoretical sciences—mathematics, physics, and metaphysics or the science of divine things —and, in addition, political or human science.

Political science is presented as the counterpart of metaphysics. Both emerge from natural science when the student of nature is forced to inquire into principles (or beings) that are beyond nature and natural things, yet are needed to explain the being of at least two of the kinds of bodies that constitute the sensible world—the heavenly bodies and man. The inquiry into the heavenly bodies forces the inquirer to acquaint himself with higher principles and shows the need for metaphysics (not politics); but it does not enable him to pursue the inquiry into the higher science to the point of explaining the being of the heavenly bodies (I, sec. 16). The need to understand the principles of reason or the intellect in man forces the inquirer again to acquaint himself with things that are higher than nature; it leads him to a point "similar" to the inquiry into the principles of the heavenly bodies. The ascent from man—from the intellect and intelligible things— proves itself a more fruitful line of inquiry into the higher principles; it enables the inquirer to come to the point of acquainting himself with these principles, from which he then descends to understand man and sublunar things (I, sec. 17). This fact is indicated by Alfarabi in the center of his account of the theoretical sciences, and it is central to the remaining portion of his account of these sciences. Henceforth, the inquiry into heavenly bodies is abandoned; man and human things become the dominant theme.

Alfarabi presents two accounts of political science. The first and slightly more extensive account is given as an extension or completion of natural science (I, secs. 17–18). Natural science is followed by metaphysics (I, sec. 19). And metaphysics, in turn, is followed by a second account of political science (I, sec. 20), which does not continue the line of inquiry pursued in metaphysics, but completes the account of politics given in natural science. In natural science, the inquirer comes to know the "ends and the ultimate perfection" of man and that man cannot reach his perfection through the natural principles that are in him and in the world of nature, but must make use of certain rational principles that are in himself and work with them toward his perfection. This leads to the discovery that man's perfection is not achieved through metaphysical beings, but through "another kind" of things, "different from the metaphysical." These are the "acts and states of character" which are formed through the exercise of the rational principles that are in man himself and that enable him to attain the perfection the knowledge of which was achieved "in natural science." Finally, it becomes evident in natural science that man by nature is a social and political animal: he cannot achieve his perfection in isolation; he needs to cooperate and associate with others, and live next to them. The investigation of the rational principles and of the "acts and states of character" by which man labors toward perfection, belongs to "another science and another inquiry," that is, to political science proper as distinguished from the foundations of political science that have formed part of natural science. The dichotomy established in natural science between metaphysics and political science, which are said to deal with things that are different "in kind," finds its application in the account of these two sciences. Metaphysics aims to know the ultimate causes of the beings. Yet the account of political science that comes next in no way depends on the results of this kind of investigation of the beings beyond and above nature; rather, it builds on the foundations provided by natural science. It investigates the things by which man reaches his perfection and distinguishes them from the things that obstruct him from reaching it—that is, the moral virtues and vices. Then it considers the structure of the city and compares it to the structure of the world, or rather to the association of the "bodies" in the totality of the world. Contrary to his accounts of the same theme in his popular political works, here Alfarabi excludes the metaphysical or divine beings from the structure of the world to which he compares the structure of the city. Not only are the foundations of political science developed in natural science, but also the central subject of political science (the city) is made to correspond to the kinds of bodies—that is, "sensible" bodies—that constitute the world, which is the main subject of natural science (cf. I, sec. 14). In both respects, Alfarabi points to the possibility of a "natural" science of human and political things that will be elaborated by Ibn Khaldūn.

Although man is said to be a natural being and the science of man is said to belong to natural science rather than to mathematics or metaphysics, political science is not reduced to, or made a part or a branch of, natural science. Man is a natural being of a special kind, and the differences between man and all other kinds of natural beings result from the difference in the way that nature prepares man to achieve his perfection. It does not give man his perfection but only the means for achieving it by himself through will and choice. Unlike the other kinds of natural beings, man is able to know the end toward which he must work as well as the means with which he performs the actions (including the organization of his social life and the exploitation of his natural environment) that bring him to that end. This knowledge is prior to, and an indispensable condition for, right action. The crucial question, however, is whether what is required for right action is primarily knowledge of all the beings or knowledge of man and human things —that is, what we have called theoretical political science. The *Attainment of Happiness* appears to waver between these two answers.

If perfect knowledge of all natural and divine beings and of their order, or perfect knowledge of the ultimate causes of all and, especially, the highest beings, is a necessary condition for right action, then political science will come after metaphysics because we must have metaphysics before we can engage in right action. Now if metaphysical knowledge were available, one would be hard put to make a case against acting on the basis of that knowledge. The possibility of the perfection of theoretical knowledge is assumed, then defended, and finally made a dominant theme in the *Philosophy of Plato and Aristotle;* and the quest for right action is always associated with and subordinated to the quest for the perfection of theoretical knowledge. But it is nowhere asserted that this theoretical perfection has been achieved, either by Plato, or by Aristotle, or by anyone else of whom Alfarabi had first-hand knowledge.

Alfarabi's *Philosophy of Plato* culminates in the city of the *Republic,* a city perfected "in speech." This city is meant to be truly just and good and to contain everything that enables its citizens to attain happiness, which requires that philosophy and the royal art come together (II, secs. 31–32). The *Republic* is then supplemented by the *Timaeus,* which deals with the place of the sciences in the city of the *Republic.* And here we learn that the science of natural and divine beings is not as yet complete and must therefore be investigated in that city for as long as it is necessary to do so (II, sec. 33; cf. III, sec. 20).

Alfarabi's Aristotle begins with the intention of resolving the paradox that had remained unsolved in Alfarabi's Plato. The view that man's perfection consists in theoretical knowledge is not self-evident and cannot be demonstrated with certainty until one achieves that theoretical perfection which is demonstrative knowledge of man and all other parts of the world. Before he comes to possess this knowledge, man has only an "opinion" regarding his own perfection and remains perplexed and torn by diverse beliefs about it. At this point, Alfarabi's Aristotle takes two decisive steps. He decides to start with the investigation of nature rather than will and choice (the subject matter of political science) on the ground that nature precedes will and choice in time and that will and choice cannot be understood without first understanding what man has by nature. And he decides to strive after knowledge that is certain or demonstrative in everything he investigates, be it natural or specifically human, on the ground that this is the only kind of knowledge on which man ought to act (III, sec. 3). Accordingly, his investigations commence with logic, which culminates in the description of the theoretical arts that constitute unqualified science or wisdom (III, sec. 9). They proceed to natural science, which culminates in the investigation of the human intellect whose perfection consists in the actual knowledge of the "theoretical intelligibles." The natural science investigated by Alfarabi's Aristotle "includes only what is included in the categories" and cannot give an account of things that are "not encompassed by the categories"— e.g., the Active Intellect and that which supplies the heavenly bodies with perpetual circular motion—yet are the ultimate principles of the bodies that constitute the world, including man (III, secs. 90–99; cf. I, secs. 16–17). Nevertheless, Alfarabi's Aristotle concludes that man's perfection is the perfection of his theoretical intellect, and that everything else in man, including the practical rational powers, are for the sake of, and in the service of, the theoretical intellect. Finally, Alfarabi's Aristotle finds it necessary to return and investigate the activities that proceed from volition and choice (or the human will), which belong to the practical intellect and by which man achieves theoretical perfection, and to distinguish the activities useful for achieving perfection from the ones that obstruct the way to it. Since in the activities that promote his perfection man makes use of or employs "instruments" and "materials" of all kinds and makes or brings about or forms beings of all kinds—inanimate as well as animate (such as plants, animals, and other human beings)—and thereby violates their own collective ends as species and their private ends as individuals, Alfarabi's Aristotle had to investigate the question whether and how man

should make use of other beings as instruments of his own perfection. This is a question to which Alfarabi finds no definitive answer in his Aristotle's natural or human science. (Cf. III, secs.
77–78, 99, with Aristotle *De Anima* ii. 4. 415b1-7; *Politics* i. 8.
1256b20–26.)

The answer to this question requires metaphysics to be a comprehensive science that supplies demonstrative knowledge of the
principles of all the beings and their ranks of order. Had Alfarabi
accepted the view that such a science was in fact available in
Aristotle's *Metaphysics*, he would have had to give an account of
this science at this stage of Aristotle's investigation. Instead, he
breaks off his account of his Aristotle's investigations with a series
of elliptical remarks. His explanation as to why his Aristotle had
to inquire into metaphysics is that his Aristotle's natural science
lacked natural "philosophy" and human or political "philosophy";
but he does not explain here what "philosophy" means or how it
differs from science. And, while he states that his Aristotle com-
menced or proceeded to inquire into and investigate the beings in
a manner different from that of "natural inquiry," he remains silent
about the details and conclusions of this investigation. In a short
comment that he appends to his Aristotle's investigations he explains
that, while the investigation of the "intelligibles" is necessary for
man's "final" perfection, the answer to the problems with which
his Aristotle "began" his investigations is necessary for realizing
the "political" activity for the sake of which man is made. But
there is also a knowledge that comes "after" this, which is investigated for two other purposes, to perfect the "human" activity for
the sake of which man is made and to perfect our defective natural
science, "since we do not possess metaphysical knowledge." The
connection implied in this "since" is far from clear. Taken in conjunction with Alfarabi's silence about the details and conclusions
of his Aristotle's *Metaphysics*, it indicates that this book did
not and perhaps was not meant to perfect Aristotle's natural science
by giving us metaphysics as a comprehensive and demonstrative
science of all the beings and their ranks of order. It indicates, further, that no one else since Aristotle had given a satisfactory account of such a science. Finally, it indicates that Alfarabi did not
consider the search for this science the most urgent order of busi-

ness after Aristotle's natural science. For the knowledge that must be investigated "after" the knowledge that is necessary for political activity is, according to Alfarabi, not metaphysics, but the knowledge that perfects the activity proper to man and perfects our knowledge of nature when or so long as we do not possess metaphysical knowledge. This knowledge is what Alfarabi calls "philosophy." Unlike Alfarabi's Plato, his Aristotle does not investigate or even speak of philosophy (just as he does not investigate or speak of happiness) but reaches out for wisdom and perfection. In concluding his *Philosophy of Aristotle* with the statement that what "must necessarily come to exist in every man in the way possible for him" is philosophy rather than wisdom, Alfarabi leads the reader back to his Plato and the account of the relation between philosophy, happiness, and the sciences, in the *Republic* and the *Timaeus,* where the question of the connection between theoretical perfection and right action is answered in a way that takes into account the fact that the investigation of the sciences has not as yet been completed.

In the *Attainment of Happiness,* Alfarabi organizes the activities of the theoretical virtues so as to make them culminate, not in metaphysics, but in political science. He concludes his plan for the investigations conducted in metaphysics with the statement "This is the divine inquiry into the beings." The corresponding statement ("This is political science") occurs in the center of his plan for the investigations conducted in human science, which concludes with the startling statement: "This, then, is theoretical perfection" (I, sec. 21). On a first view, this last statement appears to refer to all the preceding sciences. But in this case Alfarabi would have had to explain that this theoretical perfection is knowledge of all the beings. Instead, he first calls upon the reader to take another look and see what it is (and, by implication, see that it is not what theoretical perfection is reputed to be), and then goes on to explain what the reader should see: that this theoretical perfection comprises, not knowledge of all the beings with certainty, but "knowledge of the four kinds of things by which the citizens of cities and nations attain supreme happiness." And when, in the immediate sequel, he has to refer back to what is comprised in this theoretical perfection, he speaks of "theoretical affairs" rather than the "theoretical sciences" or "theoretical knowledge of the beings." The theoretical perfection of which he speaks, then, comprises knowledge of the four human things comprised by "theoretical" political science and, by extension, knowledge of the natural bodies and of the perfection of man, which were acquired in natural science and incorporated into political science.

The relation between theoretical perfection and right action appears to be resolved in the following manner. Theoretical perfection that comprises the theoretical sciences or perfect knowledge of all the beings with certainty, is the "supreme," "final," or "absolute" perfection, or happiness, that man can and must achieve (I, secs. 18, 20, 43, 52, 54). It is not, however, a necessary condition for right action, which consists in working toward that perfection by making use of the rational principles or rules that are the foundations of the human virtues and arts. Right action means to aim at the mark and presupposes knowledge of where the mark lies and of the instruments with which one aims at it. This knowledge is provided by a political science that comprises knowledge of the perfection of the theoretical virtues as well as knowledge of the deliberative virtues, moral virtues, and practical arts, with which the perfection of the theoretical virtues is to be realized. By calling this knowledge, "theoretical perfection," too, Alfarabi distinguishes between a "lower" and a "higher" theoretical perfection, makes the former the necessary condition for the pursuit of the latter, and assumes the relative independence of this knowledge and the possibility of achieving it and making it the foundation of right action, even in the absence of a comprehensive knowledge of all the beings.

Yet in the absence of a comprehensive knowledge of all the beings, this lower theoretical perfection is not, strictly speaking, available either, except by making certain assumptions (such as that nature, or God, made all the other natural beings for the sake of man and everything in man for the perfection of his theoretical intellect) with which to perfect our natural science and human science and achieve the theoretical perfection necessary for political activity. The theoretical perfection of which Alfarabi speaks at the end of his account of the theoretical sciences assumes that the perfection of man is the perfection of the theoretical virtues, ignores the problematic character of man's use of the other natural beings, and assumes that both the world of nature and the city are made up of different ranks of which the higher rules the lower and the lower serves the higher. It is followed by the assertion that the only questions that still remain concern bringing things into actual existence in conformity with this theoretical account and examining the virtues and arts by which the end is realized (I, secs. 22–37). Then, assuming the existence of a man in whom all the virtues and arts have been realized to the highest degree, Alfarabi describes the ways in which he realizes them among nations and cities (I, secs. 38–49). In this way political activity is allowed to proceed to the point where we can see with our mind's eye theoretical science ruling over nations and cities and employing all natural and human beings in its own service.

The alternative is a private pursuit of the comprehensive knowledge of all the beings which abandons political ambition and seeks the answers to the questions that have remained unanswered in natural science and human science. This pursuit is what Alfarabi at the end of his Aristotle calls perfecting the "human" activity, as distinguished from the "political" activity, for the sake of which man is made. It is an activity that is still based on the assumption that theoretical knowledge is the supreme perfection of man, but this is an assumption on which now the philosopher risks his own life, not all life. Unlike the philosopher-king, the private philosopher combines private courage with public caution. He does not presume to transform nature and human nature on the basis of an assumption that may at the end turn out to be a mere assumption.

Alfarabi remains silent about philosophy in the *Attainment of Happiness* until after the completion of the political project that unfolds in the wake of "theoretical perfection" (I, secs. 22–49). The term "philosophy" appears almost accidentally in what looks like a lexical discussion of Greek and then Arabic meanings of names connected with theoretical science that seeks to clarify the many ways in which men speak of it (I, secs. 53 ff.). The discussion immediately makes us aware of the ambiguous relationships between philosophy and theoretical perfection as the final, highest, and ruling science. After reporting on the Chaldean (i.e.,

Sabian) origin of "this science" and its transmission to the Egyptians, Greeks, Syrians, and Arabs, Alfarabi explains the names given to it by "the Greeks who possessed this science": they gave to "this science" the names "unqualified wisdom" and "highest wisdom." But he does not report what they "meant" by these names. They gave the name "science" to the acquisition of this wisdom, but again he does not explain what they meant. They gave the name "philosophy" to the scientific state of mind. He does explain that by this name they meant "the quest and the love for the highest wisdom." They gave the name "philosopher" to the one who has acquired it (presumably the highest wisdom). He explains that they meant "the one who loves and is in quest of the highest wisdom." Then he reports, not what they meant by, but the "opinion" they held about, the highest wisdom, which is that it subsumes all the virtues "potentially." Finally he reports that they gave to the highest wisdom a number of honorific names such as "wisdom of wisdoms" and "art of arts," and explains that by these names they meant the wisdom that "makes use of" all wisdoms and the art that "makes use of" all the arts (I, sec. 53). The account of the several senses in which these things are said to be, which begins here and continues to the end of the *Attainment of Happiness,* presents the reader with names and meanings and opinions expressed in names and meanings, and invites him to follow Alfarabi as he tries to sift them out and understand what "philosophy" and "philosopher" truly mean, in how many senses philosophy is related to or distinguished from religion, and in what sense the philosopher is identical with or different from the supreme ruler, the prince, the *imam,* and the lawgiver. Alfarabi reports and clarifies the meanings of these names by first accepting what they signify among the "majority of those who speak our language" (I, sec. 58). Taking language to reflect man's understanding and man's understanding to reflect the nature of things, he moves swiftly to clarify such things as the notion of the "true," "perfect," and "unqualified" philosopher, or *imam,* on the basis of generally accepted opinion and shows that he must possess all the virtues and arts and the ability to rule and make use of all others and employ them as instruments for reaching his purpose. According to this view, there cannot be a true philosopher who is not a "true" king—that is, who is not in fact a king. If the philosopher is not in fact a king, then it is only because he is a "false" philosopher whose inability to become a king and remain in power is his own fault.

Alfarabi concludes the *Attainment of Happiness* by pointing to the contradictory character of this popular view of the philosopher, which results from the failure to understand how a man's whole life can be consumed by the love and quest for the highest wisdom without actually coming to possess it for his own benefit and the benefit of others. The popular view is essentially a practical view: it cannot comprehend the idea of a permanent quest for the highest prize to which man can aspire and the apparent lack of a sense of urgency for realizing it and making use of its great potentialities. Alfarabi complicates this familiar difficulty by insisting that, if no use is made of the true philosopher who has achieved the power of benefiting others, it is not his fault but the fault of those "who either do not listen or are not of the opinion that they should listen to him" (I, sec. 62). The view of the true philosopher expressed in this statement contradicts or at least modifies radically the entire argument that had dominated in the *Attainment of Happiness* up to this point. The true philosopher is now seen as a man who possesses the art that enables him to rule, and perhaps even the arts that enable him to force others to believe that they must listen to him, and to make them actually listen to him, accept what he tells them to believe or do, obey him, help him, and become instruments of his purpose—and yet may never be actively engaged in the exercise of any of these arts. He is self-sufficient in that he can achieve his aim as true philosopher and make use of the arts he possesses for his own benefit, without being dependent on others or on external instruments and possessions. He does not refuse to exercise his arts for the benefit of others, but his philanthropy does not extend to the point of forcing others to reap the benefits of being ruled by him. He is reluctant to rule and will exercise his art for the benefit of others only with their consent and only if they come to him, listen to him, and obey him. This view of the true philosopher can be defended on the basis of the popular view. If the popular view identifies him with the true prince, *imam,* and lawgiver, and sees him as potentially the great benefactor of men, then those whose benefit will be served should seek him out, invite him to rule them, and submit to him, just as they seek out the physician who possesses the art of healing. Yet they do not, and for many reasons. They do not understand his "purpose" and see no reason why they should voluntarily help him achieve it or submit to being used as instruments in attaining it. They distrust his reluctance to rule and suspect that it results from his inability to practice the art of ruling; and they contrast his reluctance to rule to the eagerness of the physician, the *imam,* and the king to practice their arts. They understand both the private and public purposes of the physician, the *imam,* and the prince, and the benefits they hope to draw from obeying them; and their expectations of future benefits are sustained by real or imagined past benefits that they or others have received. Alfarabi counters all this with the less popular view that the prince, the *imam,* and the physician are such by virtue of their skill and art, rather than by virtue of helpers and external instruments and possessions. Yet this view is not wholly convincing because a skill or an art is formed through exercise, and its exercise requires external things with and on which it is exercised: a physician who has never found an instrument with which to exercise his skill or a sick man on whom to exercise his art can hardly be believed to possess the skill of healing or the art of medicine. If the "philosophy of the philosopher" is not wholly or largely dependent on helpers and external instruments and possessions, if the philosopher is vastly more self-sufficient than the prince, the *imam,* and the physician, it is perhaps because his art is radically different from their arts. The popular view of philosophy requires its assimilation into the art of the prince, the *imam,* and the physician. But that was not the purpose or intention of the philosophy of Plato and Aristotle which Alfarabi expounds in this book.

ALFARABI

Philosophy of
Plato and Aristotle

INTRODUCTION, 1962 EDITION

The general practice of introducing a new work by placing it in the broader context of the tradition to which it belongs encounters a peculiar difficulty in the case of Alfarabi's *Philosophy of Plato and Aristotle*. That is because this work does not conform to the current view of the Islamic philosophic tradition. This view was developed in the nineteenth century and is based on a wide range of representative works and authors. It sees Islamic philosophy as a mixture, blend, or synthesis of Aristotelian, Platonic, Neo-Platonic, and, of course, Islamic doctrines. It represents Moslem philosophers as being guided by the belief in the harmony of various philosophic and religious ideas and traditions, with little awareness of the essential heterogeneity of the elements they sought to combine. The estimates of the extent to which individual Moslem philosophers were aware of possible conflict between philosophy and religion may vary, but the prevailing view is satisfied that they were able to resolve this conflict in favor of their religious faith and the Islamic world-view. This conception of the general character of the Islamic philosophic tradition is not wholly erroneous. It was, in fact, propagated by the Moslem philosophers themselves in their effort to convince their fellow Moslems that the teachings of philosophy did not contradict the revealed teaching and that philosophic activity, far from undermining religion, was undertaken in defense of the faith.

The labor of the last generation of scholars has presented convincing evidence that the founder of this tradition was Alfarabi (al-Fārābī, ca. 870-950). But as in the case of most other Moslem philosophers, Alfarabi is known primarily through his popular and political writings—the *Harmonization of the Opinions of Plato and Aristotle*, the *Virtuous City*, the *Political Regime*, and so on—all of which seem to bear out the common view of Islamic philosophy

outlined above. This is particularly true of the first of these works.
Alfarabi was aroused by public controversies over such issues as
the creation of the world, the survival of the soul after death, and
reward and punishment in the hereafter, in which it was claimed
that the two leading philosophers had disagreed—that is, that Aristotle, unlike Plato, denied that such things were possible and hence
held views in conflict with religious beliefs. He responded by writing the *Harmonization of the Opinions of Plato and Aristotle* in
which he undertook to show that, properly understood, Aristotle's
opinions on all such issues are in agreement with those of Plato
and hence with religious beliefs. In general, exception can be taken
to Alfarabi's mode of argumentation in that work. The reasoning
is too flexible for a reader having first-hand acquaintance with the
works of Plato and Aristotle or of Alfarabi's commentaries on
them; in many instances his conclusions depend upon ones's accepting as genuine some documents of questionable authenticity,
notably the extracts from the *Enneads* of Plotinus that gained
currency in Islamic thought as the *Theology of Aristotle*. As to the
substance of his argument, it is sufficient to point out that when
the great Moslem theologian and mystic al-Ghazālī (d. 1111) set
out to expose the "intentions" of the philosophers, he refused to
pay the slightest attention to this work and was able to assert that
the real views of Aristotle and Alfarabi on these issues—that is, the
views for which they believed they had proof and that they presented in their scientific or philosophic works—were exactly the
opposite of the ones defended by Alfarabi in the *Harmonization
of the Opinions of Plato and Aristotle.*

Alfarabi's scientific or philosophic works proper—his commentaries, especially his large commentaries, on individual works
by Plato and Aristotle—which established his reputation as the
greatest philosophic authority next to Aristotle (Alfarabi was
known as the "Second Master") and which could be expected to
enlighten us on the principles underlying his popular and political
works, have always remained inaccessible to the general public,
and for the most part inaccessible even to the small scholarly circle
interested in the history of Islamic philosophy. Many of these
works seem to be lost; the ones that have survived remain for the
most part unedited and hardly ever studied; and the few that have

been edited deal with specialized subjects whose relevance to the general character of Alfarabi's thought and of Islamic philosophy is not easy to establish.

It is true that this situation can only partially be remedied by the present work, which presupposes extensive knowledge of the works of Plato and Aristotle that were available to Alfarabi and acquaintance with his specialized commentaries on them. Yet it has the distinct advantage of being Alfarabi's only comprehensive account of the philosophy of Plato and Aristotle as well as of his own views on the nature of philosophy and religion. It can, therefore, be expected to provide an answer to some of the problems raised by the works in which the harmonization of the doctrines of Plato and Aristotle through Neo-Platonism and the harmonization of philosophy and religion occupy the foreground.

To look for that answer, it is advisable to begin with the most apparent and striking features. Alfarabi presents here three separate and largely independent accounts of philosophy—one in his own name, another in the name of Plato, and a third in the name of Aristotle—without attempting to harmonize any of the doctrines or teachings of the two masters. He departs from this course in two instances. (1) At the end of the *Attainment of Happiness* (I, sec. 64) he requests the reader to make clear to himself that Plato's philosophy and Aristotle's philosophy have the same aim or purpose and that Plato and Aristotle "intended" to present the same philosophy or had the same end in view when presenting their philosophy. (2) At the beginning of the *Philosophy of Aristotle* (III, sec. 1) Alfarabi says that Aristotle had the same view of the "perfection of man" as Plato, but was dissatisfied with the lack of sufficient evidence for that view; hence he chose to "begin" from a different position, proceed differently, and so forth. Readers may differ on the interpretation of these two passages and on their significance for the understanding of Alfarabi's view of the relation between Plato and Aristotle. But Alfarabi's reticence on the area of agreement between Plato and Aristotle (as regards either their explicit or implicit doctrines) is certainly striking.

Furthermore, nowhere in the *Philosophy of Plato and Aristotle* do we find any reference to the writings, or any traces of the doctrines, commonly associated with Neo-Platonism. There is, for instance, no reference to the *Theology of Aristotle* and no trace of the theory of emanation. Many questions come to mind with respect to Alfarabi's account of some of the Platonic dialogues. We are not certain how many of them he had access to, and his account of quite a few seems rather fanciful. What is important in the present context, however, is that he nevertheless was able to re-present the entire philosophy of Plato in its political framework and that nowhere does he resort to the typically Neo-Platonic (metaphysical or mystical) interpretations of Plato in order to fill the gaps in his information.

We turn now to the more difficult issue of the relation between philosophy and religion. Since the student who attempts to clarify this issue on the basis of Alfarabi's published popular and political works must admit that it is not treated directly and explicitly in any one of them, the fact that it is so treated in the *Philosophy of Plato and Aristotle* is of particular importance, especially when it occurs in the *Attainment of Happiness* where Alfarabi presents his own views. The main argument of the *Attainment of Happiness* (I, secs. 1-49) is so constructed as to lead inevitably to a view of the relation between philosophy and religion that Alfarabi subsequently attributes to the "ancients." But throughout this argument, he does not speak of philosophy at all, and refers to religion in a single passage (I, sec. 33) and only in passing. However, in a kind of epilogue to the *Attainment of Happiness* (I, secs. 50 ff.) Alfarabi asserts that "philosophy is prior to religion in time," and explains and defends the view that "religion is an imitation of philosophy." When the term "philosophy" is introduced for the first time (I, sec. 53), it is defined as the scientific state of the soul or of the mind—the quest and love for the highest wisdom or for theoretical perfection. Alfarabi adds, however, that theoretical perfection alone is qualified, incomplete, or partial perfection, and that the man who limits himself to the theoretical sciences is not a perfect or true philosopher. The perfect philosopher, like Alfarabi's "supreme ruler," must also have the capacity for teaching all the citizens and for forming their character so as to enable everyone to achieve the happiness or perfection he is capable of attaining by nature. This, in turn, requires the ability to demonstrate as well as to persuade, to present the beings as they are as well as to represent them through images. But reverting thereafter to the restricted definition of philosophy, he now identifies it with the demonstrative knowledge of the beings, conceived in themselves, while religion is defined as the assent, secured by persuasion, to the images of these beings. Religion is an imitation of philosophy in the restricted sense inasmuch as both comprise the same subjects and both give an account of the ultimate principles of the beings, or insofar as religion supplies an imaginative account of, and employs persuasion about, things of which philosophy possesses direct and demonstrative knowledge. The conception of the relation between philosophy and religion that Alfarabi attributes to the "ancients" dissolves, however, as soon as we turn to Alfarabi's definition of perfect philosophy and of the perfect philosopher. Now a new relation emerges in which religion is part of the function of the philosopher as supreme ruler and lawgiver; it is one of the things he needs as ruler and teacher of the nonphilosophic multitude. Only the perfect philosopher *knows* the beings, represents them properly, and can judge whether the images do in fact come "as close as possible to the essences" of the things imitated. Alfarabi assigns to the philosopher a function ordinarily associated with the prophet. However, the philosopher promulgates religions by virtue of his theoretical knowledge and prudence, and through his mastery of the arts of rhetoric and poetry. The only example offered by Alfarabi in this context is what Plato does in the *Timaeus*.

Alfarabi's account of what one might call the philosophic religion leaves unanswered the more immediate question of what he thought of nonphilosophic religions or about the religions not originated by philosophers, which could not be understood as imitations of philosophy in the strict sense and which did not follow philosophy in time. Alfarabi does not discuss this question in his own name. It is, however, raised and answered in his account of the philosophy of Plato (II, sec. 7). Alfarabi's Plato begins by investigating what constitutes the perfection of man as man, which he finds to consist in a certain kind of knowledge and in a certain way of life. After finding out what that knowledge is, that man is "naturally" capable of attaining it, and that man has a faculty by which he can pursue an art that investigates that knowledge "to the point of achieving it," Alfarabi's Plato searches for the art in question and begins his search by investigating the arts "generally accepted" among the citizens of cities and nations. The first art, or group of arts, to which he turns his attention is "religious speculation," the "religious investigation of the beings," and the "religious syllogistic art." According to Alfarabi, this investigation of Plato takes place in the *Euthyphron,* a dialogue whose subject is "piety" or "that which is to be feared." But the "religious syllogistic art" recalls Islamic dialectical theology and Islamic jurisprudence rather than any of the arts investigated in the *Euthyphron.* In any case, Alfarabi's Plato is perfectly open-minded about religion and the claims of the religious arts, which is shown by the fact that he pursues three alternative investigations to discover whether they (*a*) supply the knowledge he is looking for, (*b*) do not supply it at all, or (*c*) are not adequate in this respect. Having considered these alternatives, he determines exactly "how much" knowledge these religious arts supply and concludes that the amount they supply is "not sufficient." He is thus forced to proceed and investigate other arts, until he discovers the one that is adequate and sufficient for attaining the knowledge he is seeking.

In the *Philosophy of Plato* the art in question remains nameless: it is "another" art, that is, other and higher than dialectic. In the *Philosophy of Aristotle* the art that leads to knowledge in the unqualified sense is called the "art of demonstration." Alfarabi's Aristotle, who observes a grave silence about religion, simply identifies the art of demonstration with the highest wisdom (III, sec. 9). In the *Attainment of Happiness,* too, the highest science is theoretical knowledge or the knowledge attained through the art of demonstration; the other sciences and arts that employ persuasion and imitation are given subordinate positions (I, sec. 50). Alfarabi's Aristotle, whose chief concern is to find what is self-evident or admits of demonstration, is presented as pursuing his investigations of nature and the cosmos without paying attention to the claims of the religious arts. Similarly, Alfarabi is able to offer a comprehensive account of how the citizens of cities and nations can attain the lower happiness in this life *and* the highest happiness in the world beyond by discussing only human virtues and arts. When he finally comes to speak of religion, he presents it as a subject that had already been known, defined, and assigned its proper function by the "ancients." He does not question their judgment or conclusions. The result of Plato's investigation of the religious arts in the *Euthyphron* seems to be accepted by Alfarabi's Aristotle and by Alfarabi himself as having supplied an adequate answer to the question; the cognitive value of religion is no longer in need of discussion.

On every one of these issues, the *Philosophy of Plato and Aristotle* presents a position that seems to stand in sharp contrast with, if not to contradict, Alfarabi's teachings in his popular and political works. This makes it mandatory that one should undertake a more thorough investigation of the present work and a fresh examination of the popular and political works in the light of the results of this investigation. The fact that Alfarabi's popular and political works have been accessible long before the present work should not be allowed to obscure the fact that it is here that he gives an account of the theoretical foundation on the basis of which those other works should be understood, and of the philosophic principles that are applied in the other works. Although not wholly erroneous, the generally accepted view of Alfarabi's thought and of the philosophic tradition he founded must be seen in the new perspective provided by the *Philosophy of Plato and Aristotle*.

Such readers as are not able to consult the Arabic original may be curious to know whether this version is literal and may wonder about some peculiarities of its style, especially such as are not in keeping with perfectly flowing English. It is necessary to state that in the present translation the requirement of intelligibility has been given precedence over literalness and that idiomatic niceties have been subordinated to the requirement of remaining faithful to the style of the Arabic text. This choice was imposed by the text itself. Alfarabi's style is never obscure. In many places, however, it is extremely compressed and difficult to comprehend without adequate preparation and effort. Because a translation cannot escape interpreting the original to some extent, this version may be somewhat easier to read (partly because of the divisions, symbols, and punctuation marks, none of which are to be found in the Arabic manuscripts of the text). But no effort was made to cover up the many difficulties and problems with which the text is riddled. Alfarabi's style has been justly characterized by Pico della Mirandola as *grave et meditatum*. As if to insure that the impatient reader turn away to what for him would be more profitable tasks, Alfarabi tries his patience at the very beginning of the *Attainment of Happiness*.

Philosophy of Plato and Aristotle

Part I

The Attainment of Happiness

i

1   The human things through which nations and citizens   **2**
of cities attain earthly happiness in this life and supreme happiness
in the life beyond[1] are of four kinds: theoretical virtues, deliberative virtues,[2] moral virtues, and practical arts.[3]   **5**
2   Theoretical virtues consist in[1] the sciences whose ultimate
purpose is only to make the beings and what they contain intelligible with certainty. This knowledge is in part possessed by man from
the outset without his being aware of it and without perceiving
how he acquired it or where it comes from. This is primary knowledge.[2] The rest is acquired by meditation, investigation and inference, and instruction and study. The first premises are known by   **10**
primary knowledge; on their basis one proceeds to the subsequent[2]
knowledge gained from investigation, inference, instruction, and
study. By investigation or instruction one seeks the knowledge   **3**
of things that are unknown from the outset: when they are being
investigated and their knowledge is sought, they are problems; and
afterwards when man by inference or study has been led to
conviction, opinion, or knowledge[3] about them they become conclusions.[4]
3   The attainment of certain truth is aimed at in every problem. Yet frequently we do not attain certainty. Instead we may   **5**
attain certainty about part of what we seek, and belief and
persuasion about the rest. We may arrive at an image of it or
wander from it and believe that we have encountered it without
having done so. Or we may become perplexed, as when the
arguments for and against strike us as having equal force. The
cause of this [confusion] is the variety of the methods we use in
treating a problem; for a single method could not lead us to   **10**

different convictions about problems. No, what leads us to different convictions about the many classes of problems must be various methods.[1] Unaware of their varieties or of the specific differences between them, we believe we are using the same method for every problem. Thus, although for one problem we ought to use a method that leads to certainty and for another a method with which to arrive at a similitude or image or a method that leads to persuasion and belief, we think that the method is one and the same and that the method we use in the latter case is the same as   15
the one we use in the former. Such is the situation in which we find ourselves, for the most part, and also the great majority of the speculators and investigators we see around us.[2]

    4   So let it be clear to you that before setting out to investigate problems we must realize that all these methods have to be learned as an art:[1] we must know how to distinguish the various methods by means of specific differences and marks designating each, and   4
we must have our innate and natural aptitude for science developed through an art that can provide us with knowledge of these differences since our innate capacity alone is insufficient for differentiating these methods from each other.[2] This means that we must ascertain (1) the conditions and states of the first premises and the order of their arrangement if they are to lead the investigator necessarily to the truth itself and to certainty about it; (2) the   5
conditions and states of the first premises and the order of their arrangement when they cause the investigator to wander from the truth, perplex him, and prevent him from perceiving even where the truth of his problem might lie; (3) the conditions and states of the first premises and the order of their arrangement when they provide belief and persuasion about a problem and make one even fancy that this is certainty although it is not; and (4) the conditions and states of the first premises and the order of their arrangement when they lead the investigator not to the truth   10
itself but to a similitude and image of truth.[3] Only after knowing all of this should we set out to seek knowledge of the beings by investigating them ourselves or being instructed by others. For it is only by knowing everything we have mentioned that we find out how to investigate and how to instruct and study. This [logical] faculty enables us to discern whether what we infer is certain

knowledge or mere belief, whether it is the thing itself or its image
and similitude. It enables us also to examine what we have   15
learned from others and what we ourselves teach others.

5   The primary cognitions relative to every genus of beings are
the *principles of instruction*[1] in that genus, provided they possess
the states and conditions through which the student is led to the
certain truth about what he seeks to know in the genus.[2] If all or
most of the species comprised by the genus should possess causes
by which, *from* which, or *for* which[3] these species exist, then   5
these are the *principles of being*[1] of the species comprised by the
genus, and one should attempt to know them. Now when the primary cognitions relative to some genus are identical with the
causes of the species comprised by that genus, then the principles of
instruction in it are identical with the principles of being. Demonstrations proceeding from these primary cognitions are called
demonstrations of *why* the thing is, for in addition to knowledge   5
of *whether* the thing is, they give an account of *why* it is. But
when the cognitions possessing the states and conditions [that lead
to the certain truth about what we seek to know] in a genus of
beings are the grounds of our knowledge *that* the species comprised by that genus exist, without being the grounds of the existence of any of them, then the principles of instruction in that genus
are different from the principles of being. The demonstrations
proceeding from *these* cognitions will be demonstrations of *whether*
the thing is and demonstrations of *that* it is, not demonstrations   10
of *why* it is.[4]

6   The principles of being are four:[1] (1) *What, by what,* and
how[2] the thing is—these have the same meaning [inasmuch as
they signify the *formal* cause]. (2–3) *From what*[3] it is. (4) *For
what* it is [which signifies the *final* cause]. (For by the question
from what it is we signify either [2] the *agent* principles or [3]
the *materials;*[4] whereupon the causes and principles of being
become four.) The genera of beings [may be divided into three
kinds, according to the number of their causes].[5] The first admits
of having no cause at all for its existence—this is the ultimate   15
principle for the being of all other beings regarding which we have
only the principles of *our* knowledge of it [and not the principles
of its being]. The second possesses all the four. The third admits

of having only three of them; it cannot possess the material principle.[6]

7 Every science whose sole aim is to make the beings intelligible seeks first to ascertain the presence of everything comprised by the genus[1] of which it seeks to know the species, and   **6**
next to ascertain the principles of being of the species that possess such principles and find out how many principles they possess. If they possess all the four principles, one should look for all of them rather than confine himself to some and exclude others. If they do not possess all the four, one should attempt to understand how many principles can be found in them, whether three or two or one.[2] Moreover, one should not confine himself to the proximate principles of the genus, but look for the principles of these principles, and the principles of the latter, until he arrives at the furthest principle he can find in it, at which he should come to a stop. If this ultimate principle—which is the ultimate principle with respect to this genus—also has a principle, and the latter principle is not related to this genus but to another, one   **10**
should not reach for it but set it aside, postponing the inquiry into it until he comes to inquire into the science that comprises the other genus.[3]

8   When the principles of instruction in the genus into which one inquires are identical with the principles of being of the species it comprises, he should employ the principles of instruction and proceed with the matter at hand until he covers all the species comprised. He will then know with respect to every problem both *whether* the thing is and *why* it is, until he arrives at the ultimate   **15**
principle to be reached in the genus. On the other hand, when the principles of instruction in a genus of beings are different from the principles of being (this happens only in the genus whose principles of being are obscure and not known from the outset, and whose principles of instruction are not of the same rank, but inferior to its principles of being), then the only way to get to   **7**
know the principles of being is to start from the principles of instruction and arrange them to make the conclusion follow necessarily from them. In this case the resulting conclusion is itself the source to which the principles of instruction that had been so composed and arranged owe their existence. So the principles of

instruction are here the grounds of *our knowledge* of the principles of being, while the conclusions resulting from them[1] are the
sources and the grounds of the existence of the premises that happened to be employed as principles of instruction.[2] In this manner
one ascends from knowledge of the principles of instruction,   5
which are inferior to the principles of being, to certainty about the
principles of being, which are higher. If the principle of being
upon which we come in this way has a further principle that is
still higher and more remote, we make the former into a premise
and ascend to the principle of the principle. We keep following
this course until the very ultimate principle to be found in that
genus is reached.

   9   Having ascended to a principle *B* through things (*A*, *A*₁,
*A*₂) that are known and that owe their existence to this principle,   10
it is possible that there still will be other unknown things (*A*₃, *A*₄,
. . .) that owe their existence to this principle. Originally, the
latter were hidden from us and we had no knowledge of them.
But once we employ this principle *B* (which is now known to us)
as a premise and proceed to know these other things (*A*₃, *A*₄,
. . .) that originate from it, *B* will supply us knowledge of both
whether those other things are and *why* they are. For it is possible that many things (*A*, *A*₁, *A*₂, . . .) be originated from a
single principle *B*, and that, when we begin, only one of them *A*   15
is known to us, while the principle *B* and the other things (*A*₁, *A*₂,
. . .) that originate from it remain hidden. We ascend from the one
thing *A* that we know to gain knowledge of the principle *B*, and
this one thing *A* will supply us the knowledge only *that* the principle *B* exists. Then we employ the principle *B* as a premise to explain the other hidden things (*A*₁, *A*₂, . . .) that originate from it,
and thus proceed to know both that they are and the cause of their   8
being. If this principle *B* has a further principle *C*, we employ *B*
again to explain its principle *C;* *B* will in turn supply us with the
knowledge that its higher principle *C* exists. We are thus employing
B to explain two things: in the first [that is, its principle *C*] it
supplies us with the knowledge only that it exists, while in the
second [that is, the thing(s) that originate from it, but were at
first unknown to us (*A*₁, *A*₂, . . .)] it supplies us with both the
knowledge that it exists and the cause of its being. Likewise, if the   5

principle-of-the-principle *C* is similar—in that it also has a principle *D*, and there are things (*B*₁, *B*₂, . . .) that originate from it—we employ the principle-of-the-principle *C* to explain its principle *D* as well as to explain these other hidden things (*B*₁, *B*₂, . . .) that originate from it. Whereupon this principle *C*, too, will supply us, regarding its principle *D*, with the knowledge only that it exists, and, regarding these other things (*B*₁, *B*₂, . . .), with both the knowledge that they are and the cause of their being.

10   The first genus of beings into which one should inquire   10
is that which is easier for man and in which perplexity and mental confusion are less likely to occur.[1] This is the genus of numbers and magnitudes. The science that comprises the genus of numbers and magnitudes is mathematics. One should begin first with numbers, give an account of the numbers [or units] by which things are measured, and concomitantly, an account of how numbers are used to measure the other magnitudes [or quantities][2] that can be measured. Moreover, one should give an account of   15
magnitudes: their figures, their positions, and their orderly proportion, composition, and symmetry. One should inquire into (*a*) magnitudes in which number is inherent. To these magnitudes he should attribute the measurement and orderly proportion, composition, and symmetry inherent in them because of number. These magnitudes possess the properties of measurement and orderly proportion, composition, and symmetry for two reasons: because   9
they are magnitudes and because they are numbered. (*b*) As to the magnitudes in which number is not inherent, it is only because they are magnitudes that they possess such measurement and orderly proportion, composition, or symmetry as inhere in them. Next one should inquire into all the other beings, and   5
attribute measurement and orderly proportion and symmetry to the ones in which these are inherent because of number alone. One should inquire also into all the things that possess magnitude and attribute to them everything that inheres in magnitude as magnitude, such as figures, positions, measurement, proportion, composition, and symmetry. To the things in which these mathematical properties are inherent because of both number and magnitude, he should attribute both kinds of mathematical properties, until he exhausts all the beings in which these properties   10

are present because of number and magnitude. This will also lead[3] to optics, spherics and astronomy, music, the study of weights, and mechanics.[4] One should now begin and assume everything with respect to number and magnitude that constitutes the principles of instruction in the genus into which he inquires, arrange these principles following the order obtained through the above-mentioned [logical] faculty, and seek to give an account of each   15 mathematical property present in the things into which he inquires, until he exhausts all of them or achieves in that genus the degree of knowledge necessary for elaborating the axioms of the art. One need not proceed further, because what remains is similar in kind.

11   It is characteristic of this science that inquires into numbers and magnitudes that the principles of instruction in it are identical with the principles of being. Hence all demonstrations proceeding from its principles combine the two things—I mean they give an account of the thing's existence and of why it exists: **10** all of them are demonstrations of both *that* the thing is and *why* it is. Of the principles of being, it employs [only the formal, that is] *what* the thing is and *by what* and *how* it is, to the exclusion of the other three. For numbers and magnitudes, in the mind and stripped from the material, have no principles related to their genus apart from the principles of their being just mentioned. They possess the other principles only on account of their coming   5 into being by nature or the will, that is, when they are assumed to be in materials. Since this science does not inquire into them as being in materials, it does not deal with what is extraneous to them so far as they are not in materials.[1]

12   One begins,[1] then, first with numbers [that is, arithmetic], proceeds next to magnitudes [that is, geometry], then to all things in which number and magnitude are inherent essentially (such as optics and the magnitudes in motion), and then to the heavenly bodies, music, the study of weights, and mechanics. In   10 this way one begins with things that may be comprehended and conceived irrespective of any material. He then proceeds to things that can be comprehended, conceived, and intellected by only slight reference to a material. Next, the things that can only be comprehended, conceived, and intellected with slightly more

reference to a material. He continues thus toward the things wherein number and magnitude inhere, yet that which can be intellected in them does not become intelligible except by pro- gressively greater reference to the material. This will lead him to the heavenly bodies, then music, then the study of weights and   15 mechanics, where he is forced to deal with things that become intelligible only with difficulty, or that cannot exist, except when they are in materials. One is now forced to include principles other than *what, by what,* and *how.* He has come to the borderline between the genus that does not have any other principle of being apart from *what* it is, and the genus whose species possess the four principles. It is at this point that the *natural* principles come   **11** into view.[2]

13   At this juncture one ought to set out to know the beings that possess the four principles of being: that is, the genus com- prising the beings that can be perceived by the intellect only when they are in materials. (Indeed the materials are called [by some][1] *the* natural things.) The inquirer ought to seize upon all the principles of instruction—that is, the first premises—relative to the genus consisting of *particular*[2] things. He also should look into   5 the primary knowledge he has and adopt from it whatever he recognizes as appropriate for being made into principles of instruc- tion in this science.

14   He then should begin to inquire into bodies and into things that are in bodies. The genera of bodies constitute the world and the things comprised by the world. In general, they are the genera of sensible bodies or of such bodies that possess sensible qualities: that is, the heavenly bodies; then earth, water, air, and   10 things of this kind (fire, vapor, etc.); then the stony and mineral bodies on the surface of the earth and inside it; and finally, plants, irrational animals, and rational animals. He should give an account of (*a*) the fact of the being and (*b*) all the principles of being of every one of these genera and of every one of the species of every genus: that is, in every problem relative to them, he should give an account of (*a*) the fact *that* the thing is and (*b*) *what, by what,* and *how* it is, *from what* it is, and *for what* it is.   15 In none of them is he to confine himself to its proximate principles.

Instead he should give an account of the principles of its principles
and of the principles of the principles of its principles, until he
arrives at its ultimate corporeal principles.[1]

15   The principles of instruction in most of what this science
comprises are distinct from the principles of being,[1] and it is
through the principles of instruction that one comes to know the
principles of being. For in every genus of natural things the prin-   **12**
ciples of instruction are inferior to the principles of being, since
the principles of being in such a genus are the grounds to which
the principles of instruction owe their existence. Hence the ascent
toward knowledge of the principles of being of every genus or
species can be made only through things that originate in these
principles. If these happen to be proximate principles *A* that in
turn have other principles *B,* the proximate principles *A* should
be employed as principles of instruction from which to ascend to   **5**
knowledge of their principles *B.* Then, when these principles *B*
become known, one proceeds from them to the principles of these
principles, *C,* until he arrives at the ultimate principles of
being in the genus. If, after ascending from the principles of
instruction to the principles of being and the knowledge of the
principles of being, there are (in addition to the primary
cognitions from which we ascended to the principles) other
things originating from these principles, and which are still unknown, then we proceed to use these principles of being as   **10**
principles of instruction and so come to know the other, inferior
things. In relation to the other things, our principles are now both
principles of instruction and principles of being. We follow this
procedure in every genus of sensible bodies and in each of the
species of every genus.[2]

16   When one finally comes to inquire into the heavenly
bodies and investigate the principles of their being, this inquiry   **15**
into the principles of their being will force him to look for principles that are not natures or natural things, but beings more
perfect than nature and natural things. They are also not bodies
or in bodies. Therefore one needs another kind of investigation
here and another science that inquires exclusively into beings that
are metaphysical. At this point he is again standing between two

sciences: the science of nature and [metaphysics or] the science of
what is *beyond* natural things in the order of investigation and   **13**
instruction and *above* them in the order of being.[1]

17   When his inquiry finally reaches[1] the stage of investigating
the principles of the being of animals, he will be forced to inquire
into the soul and learn about psychical [or animate] principles, and
from there ascend to the inquiry into the rational animal. As he
investigates the principles of the latter, he will be forced to inquire
into (1) *what, by what,* and *how,* (2–3) *from what,* and (4) *for*   *5*
what it is. It is here that he acquaints himself with the intellect
and things intelligible. He needs to investigate (1) *what* the
intellect is and *by what* and *how* it is, and (2–3) *from what* and
(4) *for what* it is. This investigation will force him to look for
other principles that are not bodies or in bodies, and that never
were or ever will be in bodies. This inquiry into the rational animal
will thus lead him to a similar conclusion as the inquiry into the
heavenly bodies. Now he acquaints himself with incorporeal principles that are to the beings below the heavenly bodies as those
incorporeal principles (with which he became acquainted when
investigating the heavenly bodies) are to the heavenly bodies. He   10
will acquaint himself with the principles for the sake of which
the soul and the intellect are made, and with the ends and the
ultimate perfection for the sake of which man is made. He will
know that the natural principles in man and in the world are not
sufficient for man's coming to that perfection for the sake of whose
achievement he is made. It will become evident that man needs
some rational, intellectual principles with which to work toward
that perfection.[2]

18   At this point the inquirer will have sighted another genus   15
of things, different from the metaphysical.[1] It is incumbent on man
to investigate what is included in this genus: that is, the things that
realize for man his objective through the intellectual principles
that are in him, and by which he achieves that perfection that
became known in natural science. It will become evident concomitantly that these rational principles are not mere *causes* by
which man attains the perfection for which he is made. Moreover,
he will know that these rational principles also supply many things   **14**
to natural beings other than those supplied by nature. Indeed man

arrives at the ultimate perfection (whereby he attains that which renders him truly substantial) only when he labors with these principles toward achieving this perfection. Moreover, he cannot labor toward this perfection except by exploiting a large number of   5 natural beings and until he manipulates them to render them useful to him for arriving at the ultimate perfection he should achieve.[2] Furthermore, it will become evident to him in this science that each man achieves only a portion of that perfection, and what he achieves of this portion varies in its extent, for an isolated individual cannot achieve all the perfections by himself and without the aid of many other individuals. It is the innate disposition of every man to join another human being or other men in the labor he   10 ought to perform: this is the condition of every single man. Therefore, to achieve what he can of that perfection, every man needs to stay in the neighborhood of others and associate with them.[3] It is also the innate nature of this animal to seek shelter and to dwell in the neighborhood of those who belong to the same species, which is why he is called the *social* and *political* animal. There emerges now another science and another inquiry that investigates   15 these intellectual principles and the acts and states of character with which man labors toward this perfection. From this, in turn, emerge the science of man and political science.[4]

19   He should begin to inquire into the metaphysical beings and, in treating them, use the methods he used in treating natural things. He should use as their principles of instruction the first premises that happen to be available and are appropriate to this genus, and in addition, the demonstrations of natural science that   **15** fit as principles of instruction in this genus. These should be arranged according to the order mentioned above,[1] until one covers every being in this genus. It will become evident to whoever investigates these beings that none of them can possess any material at all; one ought to investigate every one of them only as to (1) *what* and *how* it is, (2) *from what* agent and (4) *for*   5 *what* it is. He should continue this investigation until he finally reaches a being that cannot possess any of these principles at all (either *what* it is or *from what* it is or *for what* it is) but is itself the first principle of all the aforementioned beings: it is itself that *by* which, *from* which, and *for* which they are, in the most

perfect modes in which a thing can be a principle for the beings,   10
modes free from all defects. Having understood this, he should
investigate next what properties the other beings possess as a
consequence of their having *this* being as their principle and the
cause of their being. He should begin with the being whose rank is
higher than the rest (that is, the one nearest to the first principle),
until he terminates in the being whose rank is inferior to the rest
(that is, the one furthest from the first principle). He will thus
come to know the ultimate causes of the beings. This is the divine[2]
inquiry into them. For the first principle is the divinity, and the   15
principles that come after it—and are not bodies or in bodies—
are the divine principles.

20   Then he should set out next upon the science of man and
investigate the *what* and the *how* of the purpose for which man
is made, that is, the perfection that man must achieve. Then he
should investigate all the things by which man achieves this perfection or that are useful to him in achieving it. These are the good,
virtuous, and noble things. He should distinguish them from things   **16**
that obstruct his achieving this perfection. These are the evils,
the vices, and the base things.[1] He should make known *what* and
how every one of them is, and *from what* and *for what* it is,
until all of them become known, intelligible, and distinguished
from each other. This is political science.[2] It consists of knowing
the things by which the citizens of cities attain happiness through   5
political association in the measure that innate disposition equips
each of them for it. It will become evident to him that political
association and the totality that results from the association of
citizens in cities correspond to the association of the bodies that
constitute the totality of the world. He will come to see in what
are included in the totality constituted by the city and the nation
the likenesses of what are included in the total world. Just as in
the world there is a first principle, then other principles subordinate
to it, beings that proceed from these principles, other beings sub-   10
ordinate to these beings, until they terminate in the beings with
the lowest rank in the order of being, the nation or the city includes
a supreme commander, followed by other commanders,[3] followed
by other citizens, who in turn are followed by other citizens, until
they terminate in the citizens with the lowest rank as citizens and

as human beings. Thus the city includes the likenesses of the things   15
included in the total world.[4]

21   This, then, is theoretical perfection. As you see, it comprises knowledge of the four kinds of things by which the citizens
of cities and nations attain supreme happiness. What still remains
is that these four be realized and have actual existence in nations
and cities while conforming to the account of them given by the
theoretical affairs.[1]

ii

22   Do you suppose that these theoretical sciences have also
given an account of the means by which these four can be actually   **17**
realized in nations and cities, or not? They have indeed given an
account of the latter as they are perceived by the intellect. Now if
it were the case that to give an account of these things as they
are perceived by the intellect is to give an account of their [actual]
existence, it would follow that the theoretical sciences have given
an account of them as actually existent. (For instance, if it were
the case that giving an intelligible account of architecture and perceiving by the intellect what constitutes architecture and what
constitutes a building make an architect of the man who has   **5**
intellected what manner of thing the art of building is, or, if it
were the case that giving an intelligible account of a building is to
give an account of its actual existence, then the theoretical sciences
do both.) But if it is not the case that the intellection of a thing
implies its existence outside the intellect and that to give an
intelligible account of it is to give an account of its actual existence,
then, when one intends to make these four things exist, he necessarily requires something else beside theoretical science.[1]

23   That is because things perceived by the intellect are as
such free from the states and accidents that they have when they   **10**
exist outside the [thinking] soul. In what remains numerically one,
these accidents do not vary or change at all; they do vary, however, in what remains one, not numerically, but in the species.[1]
Therefore when it is necessary to make the things perceived by
the intellect and remaining one in their species exist outside the

soul, one must join to them the states and accidents that must
accompany them if they are to have actual existence outside the   15
soul. This applies to the *natural* intelligibles, which are and remain
one in their species, as well as to *voluntary* intelligibles.[2]

24   However, the natural intelligibles, which exist outside
the soul, exist from nature only, and it is by nature that they are
accompanied with their accidents.[1] As for the intelligibles that
can be made to exist outside the soul by will, the accidents and   **18**
states that accompany them when they come into being are willed
too. Now voluntary intelligibles cannot exist unless they are accompanied with these accidents and states. Since everything whose
existence is willed cannot be made to exist unless it is first known,
it follows that when one plans to bring any voluntary intelligible
into actual existence outside the soul, he must first know the states
that must accompany it when it exists.[2] Because voluntary intellig-   5
ibles do not belong to things that are one numerically, but in their
species or genus, the accidents and states that must accompany
them vary constantly, increase and decrease, and fall into combina-
tions that cannot be covered at all by invariable and unchangeable
formal rules. Indeed, for some of them no rule can be established.
For others rules can be established, but they are variable rules   10
and changeable definitions. Those for which no rule at all can be
established are the ones that vary constantly and over short periods.
The others, for which rules can be established, are those whose
states vary over long periods. Those of them that come to exist are
for the most part realized by the agency of whoever wills and
does them. Yet because of obstacles standing in their way—some
of which are natural and others voluntary, resulting from the wills   15
of other individuals—sometimes none of them at all is realized.
Furthermore, they suffer not only *temporal* variations, so that
they may exist at a certain time with accidents and states different
from those that accompany them at another time before or after;
their states also differ when they exist in different *places*. This
is evident in natural things, e.g., Man. For when it [that is, the
intelligible idea Man] assumes actual existence outside the soul,
the states and accidents in it at one time are different from those   **19**
it has at another time after or before. The same is the case with
respect to different places. The accidents and states it has when

existing in one country are different from those it has in another.
Yet, throughout, the intellect perceives Man as a single intelligible idea.[3] This holds for voluntary things as well. For instance,
Moderation, Wealth, and the like are voluntary ideas perceived   5
by the intellect. When we decide to make them actually exist,
the accidents that must accompany them at a certain time will
be different from the accidents that must accompany them at
another time, and the accidents they must have when they exist
in one nation will be different from those they must have when
existing in another. In some of them, these accidents change from
hour to hour, in others from day to day, in others from month to
month, in others from year to year, in others from decade to   10
decade, and in still others they change after many decades. Therefore, whoever should will to bring any of them into actual existence
outside the soul ought to know the variable accidents that must
accompany it in the specific period at which he seeks to bring it
into existence and in the determined place in the inhabited part of
the earth. Thus he ought to know the accidents that must accompany what is willed to exist from hour to hour, from month to   15
month, from year to year, from decade to decade, or in some other
period of determinate length, in a determined locality of large or
small size. And he ought to know which of these accidents are
common to all nations, to some nations, or to one city over a long
period, common to them over a short period, or pertain to some of
them specifically and over a short period.

25   The accidents and states of these intelligibles vary when-   **20**
ever certain events occur in the inhabited part of the earth, events
common to all of it, to a certain nation or city, or to a certain
group within a city, or pertaining to a single man. Such events are
either natural or willed.

26   Things of this sort are not covered by the theoretical
sciences, which cover only the intelligibles that do not vary at all.[1]
Therefore another faculty and another skill is required with which   5
to discern the voluntary intelligibles, [not as such, but] insofar as
they possess these variable accidents: that is, the modes according
to which they can be brought into actual existence by the will at
a determined time, in a determined place, and when a determined
event occurs. That is the *deliberative* faculty.[2] It is the skill and

the faculty by which one discovers and discerns the variable accidents of the intelligibles whose particular instances are made to
exist by the will, when one attempts to bring them into actual exist-   10
ence by the will at a determined time, in a determined place, and
when a determined event takes place, whether the time is long or
short, whether the locality is large or small.

27   Things are *discovered* by the deliberative faculty only
insofar as they are found to be useful for the attainment of an end
and purpose.[1] The discoverer first sets the end before himself and
then investigates the means by which that end and that purpose are   15
realized. The deliberative faculty is most perfect when it discovers
what is most useful for the attainment of these ends. The ends may
be truly good, may be evil, or may be only believed to be good.[2] If
the means discovered are the most useful for a virtuous end, then
they are noble and fair. If the ends are evil, then the means dis-   **21**
covered by the deliberative faculty are also evil, base, and bad.
And if the ends are only believed to be good, then the means
useful for attaining and achieving them are also only believed to
be good. The deliberative faculty can be classified accordingly.   5
Deliberative *virtue* is that by which one discovers what is most useful for some virtuous end. As for the deliberative faculty by which
one discovers what is most useful for an evil end, it is not a
deliberative *virtue* but ought to have other names.[3] And if the
deliberative faculty is used to discover what is most useful for
things that are only believed to be good, then that deliberative
faculty is only believed to be a deliberative virtue.

28   (1) There is a certain deliberative virtue that enables one   10
to excel in the discovery of what is most useful for a virtuous end
common to many nations, to a whole nation, or to a whole city,
at a time when an event occurs that affects them in common.[1]
(There is no difference between saying *most useful for a virtuous
end* and *most useful and most noble,* because what is both most
useful and most noble necessarily serves a virtuous end, and what
is most useful for a virtuous end is indeed the most noble with
respect to that end.) This is *political* deliberative virtue. The
events that affect them in common may persist over a long period   15
or vary within short periods. However, *political* deliberative virtue
is the deliberative virtue that discovers the most useful and most

noble that is common to many nations, to a whole nation, or to a whole city, irrespective of whether what is discovered persists there for a long period or varies over a short period. When it is concerned exclusively with the discovery of the things that are common to many nations, to a whole nation, or to a whole city, and that **22** do not vary except over many decades or over longer periods of determinate length, then it is more akin to a legislative ability.[2] (2) The deliberative virtue with which one discovers only what varies over short periods. This is the faculty that manages the different classes of particular, temporary tasks in conjunction with, and at the occurrence of, the events that affect all nations, a cer- **5** tain nation, or a certain city. It is subordinate to the former.[3] (3) The faculty by which one discovers what is most useful and noble, or what is most useful for a virtuous end, relative to one group among the citizens of a city or to the members of a household. It consists of a variety of deliberative virtues, each associated with the group in question: for instance, it is *economic* deliberative virtue or *military* deliberative virtue. Each of these, in turn, is subdivided inasmuch as what it discovers (*a*) does not vary except over long periods or (*b*) varies over short periods. (4) The deliber- **10** ative virtue may be subdivided into still smaller fractions, such as the virtue by which one discovers what is most useful and noble with respect to the purpose of particular arts or with respect to particular purposes that happen to be pursued at particular times. Thus it will have as many subdivisions as there are arts and ways of life. (5) Furthermore, this faculty can be divided also insofar as (*a*) it enables man to excel in the discovery of what is **15** most useful and noble with respect to his own end when an event occurs that concerns him specifically, and (*b*) it is a deliberative virtue by which he discovers what is most useful and noble with respect to a virtuous end to be attained by somebody else—the latter is *consultative* deliberative virtue.[4] These two may be united in a single man or may exist separately.

　　29　It is obvious that the one who possesses a virtue by which he discovers what is most useful and noble, and this for the sake of a virtuous end that is good (irrespective of whether what is discovered is a true good that he wishes for himself, a true good **23** that he wishes someone else to possess, or something that is

believed to be good by whomever he wishes it for), cannot possess this faculty without possessing a moral virtue.[1] For if a man
wishes the good for others, then he is either truly good or else
believed to be good by those for whom he wishes the good although
he is not good and virtuous. Similarly he who wishes the true good   5
for himself has to be good and virtuous, not in his deliberation, but
in his moral character and in his acts. It would seem that his
virtue, moral character, and acts, have to correspond to his power
of deliberation and ability to discover what is most useful and
noble. Hence if he discovers by his deliberative virtue only those
most useful and noble means that are of great force (such as
what is most useful for a virtuous end common to a whole nation,
to many nations, or to a whole city, and does not vary except over   10
a long period), then his moral virtues ought to be of a comparable
measure. Similarly, if his deliberative virtues are confined to means
that are most useful for a restricted end when a specific event
occurs, then this is the measure of his [moral] virtue also. Accordingly, the more perfect the authority and the greater the power of
these deliberative virtues, the stronger the authority and the   15
greater the power of the moral virtues that accompany them.
      30 (1) Since the deliberative virtue by which one discovers
what is most useful and noble with respect to the ends that do not
vary except over long periods and that are common to many
nations, to a whole nation, or to a whole city when an event that
affects them in common occurs, has more perfect authority and
greater power, the virtues that accompany it should possess the
most perfect authority and the greatest power. (2) Next follows the deliberative virtue with which one excels in the dis-   **24**
covery of what is most useful for a common, though temporary,
end, over short periods; the virtues that accompany it are of
a comparable rank. (3) Then follow the deliberative virtues
confined to individual parts of the city—the warriors, the rich,   5
and so forth; the moral virtues that have to do with these parts
are of a comparable rank. (4) Finally, one comes to the deliberative virtues related to single arts (taking into account the
purposes of these arts) and to single households and single human
beings within single households (with attention to what pertains
to them as events follow one another hour after hour or day

after day); they are accompanied by a virtue of a comparable rank.

31   Therefore one ought to investigate which virtue is the   10
perfect and most powerful virtue.[1] Is it the combination of all the
virtues?; or, if one virtue (or a number of virtues) turns out to
have a power equal to that of all the virtues together, what ought
to be the distinctive mark of the virtue that has this power and is
hence the most powerful virtue? This virtue is such that when a
man decides to fulfill its functions, he cannot do so without making
use of the functions of all the other virtues. If he himself does not   15
happen to possess all of these virtues—in which case he cannot
make use of the functions of particular virtues present in him
when he decides to fulfill the functions of that virtue—that virtue
of his will be a moral virtue in the exercise of which he exploits
the acts of the virtues possessed by all others, whether they are
nations, cities within a nation, groups within a city, or parts within
each group. This, then, is the leading virtue that is not surpassed
by any other in authority. Next follow the virtues that resemble   **25**
this one in that they have a similar power with respect to single
parts of the city. For instance, together with the deliberative
faculty by which he discovers what is most useful and noble with
respect to that which is common to warriors, the general ought to
possess a moral virtue. When he decides to fulfill the functions of
the latter, he exploits the virtues possessed by the warriors as   5
warriors. His courage, for instance, ought to be such as to enable
him to exploit the warriors' particular acts of courage. Similarly,
the one who possesses a deliberative virtue by which he discovers
what is most useful and noble for the ends of those who acquire
wealth in the city ought to possess the moral virtue that enables
him to exploit the particular virtues of the classes of people
engaged in acquiring wealth.

32   The arts, too, ought to follow this pattern. The leading   10
art that is not surpassed by any other in authority is such that when
we decide to fulfill its functions, we are unable to do so without
making use of the functions of all the arts. It is the art for the fulfillment of whose purpose we require all the other arts. This, then,
is the leading art and the most powerful of the arts—just as the   15
corresponding moral virtue was the most powerful of all the moral
virtues. It is then followed by the rest of the arts. An art of a

certain class among them is more perfect and more powerful than the rest in its class if its end can be fulfilled only by making use of the functions of the other arts in its class. Such is the status of the leading military arts. For instance, the art of commanding armies is such that its purpose can be achieved only by making use of the functions of the particular arts of warfare. Similarly, the lead- **26** ing art of wealth in the city is such that its purpose with regard to wealth can be achieved only by exploiting the particular arts of acquiring wealth. This is the case also in every other major part of the city.

33 Furthermore, it is obvious that what is most useful and noble is in every case either most noble according to generally accepted[1] opinion, most noble according to a particular religion,[2] **5** or truly most noble. Similarly, virtuous ends are either virtuous and good according to generally accepted opinion, virtuous and good according to a particular religion, or truly virtuous and good. No one can discover what is most noble according to the followers of a particular religion unless his moral virtues are the specific virtues of that religion. This holds for everyone else;[3] it applies to the more powerful virtues as well as to the more particular and less powerful. Therefore the most powerful deliberative virtue and **10** the most powerful moral virtue are inseparable from each other.

34 It is evident that the deliberative virtue with the highest authority can only be subordinate to the theoretical virtue; for it merely discerns the accidents of the intelligibles that, prior to having these accidents as their accompaniments, are acquired by the theoretical virtue.[1] If it is determined that the one who possesses the deliberative virtue should discover the variable accidents and states of only those intelligibles of which he has personal in- **15** sight and personal knowledge (so as not to make discoveries about things that perhaps ought not to take place), then the deliberative virtue cannot be separated from the theoretical virtue. It follows that the theoretical virtue, the leading deliberative virtue, the leading moral virtue, and the leading [practical] art are inseparable from each other; otherwise the latter [three] will be unsound, imperfect, and without complete authority.

35 But if, after the theoretical virtue has caused the intellect **27** to perceive the moral virtues, the latter can only be made to exist

if the deliberative virtue discerns them and discovers the accidents
that must accompany their intelligibles so that they can be brought
into existence, then the deliberative virtue is anterior to the moral
virtues. If it is anterior to them, then he who possesses the delibera-   5
tive virtue discovers by it only such moral virtues as exist independently of the deliberative virtues. Yet if the deliberative virtue
is independent of the moral virtue, then he who has the capacity
for discovering the (good) moral virtues will not himself be good,
not even in a single virtue.[1] But if he himself is not good, how then
does he seek out the good or wish the true good for himself or for
others? And if he does not wish the good, how is he capable of
discovering it without having set it before himself as an end? There-   10
fore, if the deliberative virtue is independent of the moral virtue, it
is not possible to discover the moral virtue with it. Yet if the moral
virtue is inseparable from the deliberative, and they coexist, how
could the deliberative virtue discover the moral and join itself to
it? For if they are inseparable, it will follow that the deliberative
virtue did not discover the moral virtue; while if the deliberative
virtue did discover the moral virtue, it will follow that the deliberative virtue is independent of the moral virtue. Therefore either the
deliberative virtue itself is the virtue of goodness, or one should   15
assume that the deliberative virtue is accompanied by some other
virtue, different from the moral virtue that is discovered by the
deliberative faculty. If that other moral virtue is formed by the will
also, it follows that the deliberative virtue discovered it—thus the
original doubt recurs. It follows, then, that there must be some
other moral virtue—other, that is, than the one discovered by the
deliberative virtue—which accompanies the deliberative virtue and
enables the possessor of the deliberative virtue to wish the good
and the virtuous end. *That* virtue must be *natural* and must come   **28**
into being by nature, and it must be coupled with a certain deliberative virtue [that is, *cleverness*] which comes into being by nature
and discovers the moral virtues formed by the will. The virtue
formed by the will will then be the *human*[2] virtue by which man,
after acquiring it in the way in which he acquires voluntary things,
acquires the *human* deliberative virtue.[3]

36   But one ought to inquire what manner of thing that   5
natural virtue is. Is it or is it not identical with this voluntary

virtue? Or ought one to say that it *corresponds* to this virtue, like
the states of character that exist in irrational animals?—just
as it is said that courage resides in the lion, cunning in the fox,
shiftiness in the bear, thievishness in the magpie, and so on. For
it is possible that every man is innately so disposed that his soul has
a power such that he generally moves more easily in the direction
of the accomplishment of a certain virtue or of a certain state of   10
character than in the direction of doing the opposite act. Indeed
man moves first in the direction in which it is easier for him to
move, provided he is not compelled to do something else. For
instance, if a man is innately so disposed that he is more prone to
stand his ground against dangers than to recoil before them, then
all he needs is to undergo the experience a sufficient number of
times and this state of character becomes voluntary. Prior to this,
he possessed the corresponding *natural* state of character.[1] If this 15
is so in particular moral virtues that accompany particular deliberative virtues, it must also be the case with the highest moral virtues
that accompany the highest deliberative virtues. If this is so, it
follows that there are some men who are innately disposed to a
[*natural* moral] virtue that corresponds to the highest [*human*
moral] virtue[2] and that is joined to a naturally superior deliberative power, others just below them, and so on. If this is so, then   **29**
not every chance human being will possess art, moral virtue, and
deliberative virtue with great power.

37   Therefore the prince occupies his place by nature and not
merely by will.[1] Similarly, a subordinate occupies his place primarily by nature and only secondarily by virtue of the will, which
perfects his natural equipments. This being the case, the theoretical virtue, the highest deliberative virtue, the highest moral virtue,   5
and the highest practical art are realized in those equipped
for them by nature: that is, in those who possess superior natures
with very great potentialities.[2]

iii

38   After these four things are realized in a certain man, the
realization of the particular instances[1] of them in nations and

cities still remains; his knowing how to make these particular
instances exist in nations and cities remains: he who possesses such
a great power ought to possess the capacity of realizing the par-   10
ticular instances of it in nations and cities.

39 There are two primary methods of realizing them: instruction and the formation of character.¹ To instruct is to introduce the theoretical virtues in nations and cities. The formation of
character is the method of introducing the moral virtues and
practical arts in nations. Instruction proceeds by speech alone.
The formation of character proceeds through habituating nations
and citizens in doing the acts that issue from the practical states   15
of character by arousing in them the resolution to do these acts;
the states of character and the acts issuing from them should come
to possess their souls, and they should be as it were enraptured
by them.² The resolution to do a thing may be aroused by
speech or by deed.

40 Instruction in the theoretical sciences should be given
either to the *imams*¹ and the princes, or else to those who should
preserve the theoretical sciences. The instruction of these two
groups proceeds by means of identical approaches. These are the
approaches stated above.² First, they should know the first   **30**
premises and the primary knowledge relative to every kind of
theoretical science. Then they should know the various states of
the premises and their various arrangements as stated before, and
be made to pursue the subjects that were mentioned.³ (Prior to
this, their souls must have been set aright through the training
befitting the youths whose natures entitle them to this rank in the   5
order of humanity.) They should be habituated to use all the
logical methods in all the theoretical sciences. And they should be
made to pursue a course of study and form the habits of character
from their childhood until each of them reaches maturity, in
accordance with the plan described by Plato.⁴ Then the princes
among them will be placed in subordinate offices and promoted
gradually through the ranks until they are fifty years old. Then   10
they will be placed in the office with the highest authority. This,
then, is the way to instruct this group; they are the elect who should
not be confined to what is in conformity with unexamined common
opinion.⁵ Until they acquire the theoretical virtues, they ought to

be instructed in things theoretical by means of persuasive methods. They should comprehend[6] many theoretical things by way of imagining them. These are the things—the ultimate principles and the incorporeal principles—that a man cannot perceive by his intellect except after knowing many other things. The vulgar ought to comprehend merely the similitudes of these principles, which should be established in their souls by persuasive arguments. One should draw a distinction between the similitudes that ought to be presented to every nation, and in which all nations and all the citizens of every city should share, and the ones that ought to be presented to a particular nation and not to another, to a particular city and not to another, or to a particular group among the citizens of a city and not to another. All these [persuasive arguments and similitudes] must be discerned by the deliberative virtue.

41   They [the princes, *imams,* etc.] should be habituated in the acts of the practical[1] virtues and the practical arts by either of two methods. First, by means of persuasive arguments, passionate arguments, and other arguments that establish these acts and states of character in the soul completely so as to arouse the resolution to do the acts willingly. This method is made possible by the practice of the logical arts—to which the mind is naturally inclined—and by the benefits derived from such practice. The other method is compulsion.[2] It is used with the recalcitrant and the obstinate among those citizens of cities and nations who do not rise in favor of what is right willingly and of their own accord or by means of arguments, and also with those who refuse to teach others the theoretical sciences in which they are engaged.

42   Now since the virtue or the art of the prince is exercised by exploiting the acts of those who possess the particular virtues and the arts of those who practice the particular arts, it follows necessarily that the virtuous and the masters of the arts whom he [the prince] employs to form the character of nations and citizens of cities comprise two primary groups: a group employed by him to form the character of whosoever is susceptible of having his character formed willingly, and a group employed by him to form the character of those who are such that their character can be formed only by compulsion. This is analogous to what heads of households and superintendents of children and youths do.[1] For

the prince forms the character of nations and instructs them, just as the head of a household forms the character of its members and instructs them, and the superintendent of children and youths forms their character and instructs them. Just as each of the latter two forms the character of some of those who are in his custody by **32** being gentle to them and by persuasion and forms the character of others by compulsion, so does the prince. Indeed it is in virtue of the very same skill in [all three] classes of men who form the character of others and superintend them undertake both the compulsory formation of character and the formation of character received willingly; the skill varies only with respect to its degree and the extent of its power.[2] Thus the power required for forming the character of nations and for superintending them is greater than the power required for forming the character of children and 5 youths or the power required by heads of households for forming the character of the members of a household. Correspondingly, the power of the princes who are the superintendents of nations and cities and who form their character, and the power of whomever and whatever they employ in performing this function, are greater. The prince needs the most powerful skill for forming the character of others with their consent and the most powerful skill for forming their character by compulsion.

43 The latter is the craft of war: that is, the faculty that enables him to excel in organizing and leading armies and utiliz- 10 ing war implements and warlike people to conquer the nations and cities that do not submit to doing what will procure them that happiness for whose acquisition man is made. For every being is made to achieve the ultimate perfection it is susceptible of achieving according to its specific place in the order of being. Man's specific perfection is called *supreme happiness*,[1] and to each man, according to his rank in the order of humanity, belongs the specific 15 supreme happiness pertaining to his kind of man.[2] The warrior who pursues this purpose is the just warrior, and the art of war that pursues this purpose is the just and virtuous art of war.[3]

44 The other group, employed to form the character of nations and the citizens of cities with their consent, is composed of those who possess the logical virtues and arts. For it is obvious that the prince needs to return to the theoretical, intelligible things

whose knowledge was acquired by certain demonstrations, look for   33
the persuasive methods that can be employed for each, and seek
out all the persuasive methods that can be employed for it (he can
do this because he possesses the power to be persuasive about individual cases). Then he should repair to these very same theoretical things and seize upon their similitudes. He ought to make
these similitudes produce images of the theoretical things for all   5
nations jointly, so establish the similitudes that persuasive methods can cause them to be accepted, and exert himself throughout
to make both the similitudes and the persuasive methods such that
all nations and cities may share in them. Next he needs to enumerate the acts of the particular practical virtues and arts that fulfill
the above-mentioned requirements.[1] He should devise meth-   10
ods of political oratory with which to arouse the resolution to such
acts [in nations and cities]. He should employ here (1) arguments
that support [the rightness of] his own character; (2) passionate
and moral arguments that cause (a) the souls of the citizens to
grow reverent, submissive, muted, and meek. But with respect to
everything contrary to these acts he should employ passionate and
moral arguments by which (b) the souls of the citizens grow confident, spiteful, insolent, and contemptuous. He should employ
these same two kinds of arguments [a and b], respectively, with
the princes who agree with him and with those who oppose him,
with the men and the auxiliaries employed by him and with the   15
ones employed by those who oppose him, and with the virtuous
and with those who oppose them. Thus with respect to his own
position he should employ arguments by which souls grow reverent
and submissive. But with respect to his opponents he should employ arguments that cause souls to grow spiteful, insolent, and
contemptuous; arguments with which he contradicts, using persuasive methods, those who disagree with his own opinions and
acts; and arguments that show the opinions and acts of the op-
ponent as base and make their meanness and notoriety apparent.[2]
He should employ here both classes of arguments: I mean the   34
class that should be employed periodically, daily, and temporarily,
and not preserved, kept permanently, or written down; and the
other class, which should be preserved and kept permanently, or-
ally and in writing. [The latter should be kept in two Books, a

Book of Opinions and a Book of Acts.] He should place in these two Books the opinions and the acts that nations and cities were called upon to embrace, the arguments by which he sought to preserve among them and to establish in them the things they were   5 called upon to embrace so that they will not be forgotten, and the arguments with which he contradicts the opponents of these opinions and acts. Therefore the sciences that form the character of nations and cities will have three ranks of order [the first belongs to the theoretical sciences themselves, the second to the popular theoretical sciences, and the third to the image-making theoretical sciences]. Each kind will have a group to preserve it, who should be drawn from among those who possess the faculty that enables them to excel in the discovery of what had not been clearly stated to them with reference to the science they preserve, to defend it, to contradict what contradicts it, and to excel in teaching all of this to others. In all of this they should aim at accomplishing the purpose of the supreme ruler with respect to   10 nations and cities.[3]

45   Then he [the supreme ruler] should inquire next into the different classes of nations by inquiring into every nation and into the human states of character and the acts for which all nations are equipped by that nature which is common to them, until he comes to inquire into all or most nations. He should inquire into that in which all nations share—that is, the *human nature* common to them—and then into all the things that pertain specifically to every group within every nation.[1] He should discern all of these,   15 draw up an actual—if approximate—list of the acts and the states of character with which every nation can be set aright and guided toward happiness, and specify the classes of persuasive arguments (regarding both the theoretical and the practical virtues) that ought to be employed among them.[2] He will thus set down what every nation is capable of, having subdivided every nation and inquired whether or not there is a group fit for preserving the theoretical sciences and others who can preserve the popular theo-   **35** retical sciences or the image-making theoretical sciences.[3]

46   Provided all of these groups exist in nations, four sciences will emerge. First, the theoretical virtue through which the beings become intelligible with certain demonstrations. Next, these same

intelligibles acquired by persuasive methods. Subsequently, the science that comprises the similitudes of these intelligibles, accepted by persuasive methods. Finally, the sciences extracted from these three for each nation. There will be as many of these extracted sciences as there are nations, each containing everything by which a particular nation becomes perfect and happy.

47   Therefore he [the supreme ruler] has to find certain groups of men or certain individuals who are to be instructed in what causes the happiness of particular nations, who will preserve   10
what can form the character of a particular nation alone, and who will learn the persuasive methods that should be employed in forming the character of that nation. The knowledge which that nation ought to have must be preserved by a man or a group of men also possessing the faculty that enables them to excel in the discovery of what was not actually given to this man or this group of men but is, nevertheless, of the same kind for which they act as custodians, enables them to defend it and contradict what opposes it, and to excel in the instruction of that nation.¹ In all of this   15
they should aim at accomplishing what the supreme ruler had in mind for the nation, for whose sake he gave this man or this group of men what was given to them. Such are the men who should be employed to form the character of nations with their consent.

48   The best course is that each member of the groups to which the formation of the character of nations is delegated should possess a warlike virtue and a deliberative virtue for use in case there is need to excel in leading troops in war; thus every one of   **36**
them will possess the skill to form the nations' character by both methods. If this combination does not happen to exist in one man, then he [the supreme ruler] should add to the man who forms the character of nations with their consent another who possesses this craft of war. In turn, the one to whom the formation of the character of any nation is delegated should also follow the custom of employing a group of men to form the character of the nation with its consent or by compulsion, by either dividing them into two   5
groups or employing a single group that possesses a skill for doing both. Subsequently, this one group, or the two groups, should be subdivided, and so on, ending in the lowest divisions or the ones with the least power in the formation of character. The ranks

within these groups should be established according to the deliberative virtue of each individual: that is, depending on whether his
deliberative virtue exploits subordinate ones or is exploited by
one superior to it. The former will rule and the latter have a sub-   10
ordinate office according to the power of their respective deliberative virtues.[1] When these two groups are formed in any nation or
city, they, in turn, will order the rest.

49   These, then, are the modes and the methods through
which the four human things by which supreme happiness is
achieved are realized in nations and cities.

iv

50   Foremost among all of these [four] sciences[1] is that which
gives an account of the beings as they are perceived by the
intellect with certain demonstrations. The others merely take these   15
same beings and employ persuasion about them or represent them
with images so as to facilitate the instruction of the multitude of
the nations and the citizens of cities. That is because nations and
the citizens of cities are composed of some who are the elect and
others who are the vulgar. The vulgar confine themselves, or should
be confined, to theoretical cognitions that are in conformity with
unexamined common opinion.[2] The elect do not confine themselves   **37**
in any of their theoretical cognitions to what is in conformity with
unexamined common opinion but reach their conviction and knowledge on the basis of premises subjected to thorough scrutiny. Therefore whoever thinks that he is not confined to what is in conformity with unexamined common opinion in his inquiries, believes that in them he is of the "elect" and that everybody else is
vulgar. Hence the competent practitioner of every art comes to be
called one of the "elect" because people know that he does not
confine himself, with respect to the objects of his art, to what
is in conformity with unexamined opinion, but exhausts them
and scrutinizes them thoroughly. Again, whoever does not hold a
political office or does not possess an art that establishes his claim
to a political office, but either possesses no art at all or is enabled

by his art to hold only a subordinate office in the city, is said to   10
be "vulgar"; and whoever holds a political office or else possesses
an art that enables him to aspire to a political office is of the
"elect." Therefore, whoever thinks that he possesses an art that
qualifies him for assuming a political office or thinks that his position has the same status as a political office (for instance, men
with prominent ancestors and many who possess great wealth),
calls himself one of the "elect" and a "statesman."

    51   Whoever has a more perfect mastery of the art that   15
qualifies him for assuming an office is more appropriate for inclu-
sion among the elect. Therefore it follows that the most elect of
the elect is the supreme ruler. It would appear that this is so
because he is the one who does not confine himself in anything
at all to what is in conformity with unexamined common opinion.
He must hold the office of the supreme ruler and be the most elect
of the elect because of his state of character and skill. As for the
one who assumes a political office with the intention of accomplish-   **38**
ing the purpose of the supreme ruler, he *adheres* to thoroughly
scrutinized opinions. However, the opinions that caused him to
become an adherent[1] or because of which he was convinced that
he should use his art to serve the supreme ruler were based
on mere conformity to unexamined opinions; he conforms
to unexamined common opinion in his theoretical cognitions as
well. The result is that the supreme ruler and he who possesses   5
the science that encompasses the intelligibles with certain demonstrations belong to the elect. The rest are the vulgar and the
multitude. Thus the methods of persuasion and imaginative repre-
sentation are employed only in the instruction of the vulgar and
the multitude of the nations and the cities, while the certain
demonstrative methods, by which the beings themselves are made
intelligible, are employed in the instruction of those who belong
to the elect.

    52   This is the superior science and the one with the most   10
perfect [claim to rule or to] authority. The rest of the authoritative
sciences are subordinate to this science. By *the rest of the authoritative sciences* I mean the second and the third, and that which is
derived from them,[1] since these sciences merely follow the example
of that science and are employed to accomplish the purpose of

that science, which is supreme happiness and the final perfection
to be achieved by man.[2]

53   It is said that this science existed anciently among the
Chaldeans,[1] who are the people of al-Irāq,[2] subsequently reaching   15
the people of Egypt,[3] from there transmitted to the Greeks,
where it remained until it was transmitted to the Syrians[4] and
then to the Arabs. Everything comprised by this science was
expounded in the Greek language, later in Syriac, and finally in
Arabic. The Greeks who possessed this science used to call it "unqualified" *wisdom* and the *highest wisdom*. They called the acquisition of it *science*, and the scientific state of mind *philosophy* (by
which they meant the quest and the love for the highest wisdom).
They called the one who acquires it *philosopher* (meaning the one
who loves and is in quest of the highest wisdom). They held that   **39**
potentially it subsumes all the virtues. They called it the *science of
sciences*, the *mother of sciences*, the *wisdom of wisdoms*, and
the *art of arts* (they meant the art that makes use of all the
arts, the virtue that makes use of all the virtues, and the wisdom
that makes use of all wisdoms). Now "wisdom" may be used   5
for consummate and extreme competence in any art whatsoever
when it leads to performing feats of which most practitioners of
that art are incapable.[5] Here wisdom is used in a qualified sense.[6]
Thus he who is extremely competent in an art is said to be "wise"
in that art. Similarly, a man with penetrating practical judgment
and acumen may be called "wise" in the thing regarding which he
has penetrating practical judgment. However, unqualified wisdom
is this science and state of mind alone.[7]

54   When the theoretical sciences are isolated and their pos-   10
sessor does not have the faculty for exploiting them for the benefit
of others, they are defective philosophy.[1] To be a truly perfect
philosopher one has to possess both the theoretical sciences and
the faculty for exploiting them for the benefit of all others according to their capacity. Were one to consider the case of the true
philosopher, he would find no difference between him and the
supreme ruler. For he who possesses the faculty for exploiting what
is comprised by the theoretical matters for the benefit of all others
possesses the faculty for making such matters intelligible as well   15
as for bringing into actual existence those of them that depend on
the will. The greater his power to do the latter, the more perfect
is his philosophy. Therefore he who is truly perfect possesses

with sure insight, first, the theoretical virtues, and subsequently
the practical.[2] Moreover, he possesses the capacity for bringing
them about in nations and cities in the manner and the measure
possible with reference to each. Since it is impossible for him to
possess the faculty for bringing them about except by employing
certain demonstrations, persuasive methods, as well as methods   **40**
that represent things through images, and this either with the consent of others or by compulsion, it follows that the true philosopher
is himself the supreme ruler.

55   Every instruction is composed of two things: (*a*) making
what is being studied comprehensible[1] and causing its idea to be
established in the soul and (*b*) causing others to assent[1] to what
is comprehended and established in the soul. There are two ways   5
of making a thing comprehensible: first, by causing its essence to
be perceived by the intellect, and second, by causing it to be
imagined through the similitude that imitates it. Assent, too, is
brought about by one of two methods, either the method of certain
demonstration or the method of persuasion. Now when one
acquires knowledge of the beings or receives instruction in them, if
he perceives their ideas themselves with his intellect, and his
assent to them is by means of certain demonstration, then the
science that comprises these cognitions is *philosophy*. But if they
are known by imagining them through similitudes that imitate   10
them, and assent to what is imagined of them is caused by persuasive methods, then the ancients call what comprises these
cognitions *religion*.[2] And if those intelligibles themselves are
adopted, and *persuasive* methods are used, then the religion com-
prising them is called *popular, generally accepted,* and *external*
philosophy.[3] Therefore, according to the ancients, religion is an
imitation of philosophy.[4] Both comprise the same subjects and
both give an account of the ultimate principles of the beings. For   15
both supply knowledge about the first principle and cause of the
beings, and both give an account of the ultimate end for the sake
of which man is made—that is, supreme happiness—and the
ultimate end of every one of the other beings. In everything of
which philosophy gives an account based on intellectual perception
or conception, religion gives an account based on imagination. In
everything demonstrated by philosophy, religion employs per-

suasion. Philosophy gives an account of the ultimate principles (that is, the essence of the first principle and the essences of the incorporeal second principles[5]), as they are perceived by the **41** intellect. Religion sets forth their images by means of similitudes of them taken from corporeal principles and imitates them by their likenesses among political offices.[6] It imitates the divine acts by means of the functions of political offices.[6] It imitates the actions of natural powers and principles by their likenesses among the faculties, states, and arts that have to do with the will, just as Plato does in the *Timaeus*.[7] It imitates the intelligibles by their **5** likenesses among the sensibles: for instance, some imitate *matter* by *abyss* or *darkness* or *water,* and *nothingness* by *darkness*. It imitates the classes of supreme happiness—that is, the ends of the acts of the human virtues—by their likenesses among the goods that are believed to be the ends. It imitates the classes of true happiness by means of the ones that are believed to be happiness. It imitates the ranks of the beings by their likenesses among **10** spatial and temporal ranks. And it attempts to bring the similitudes of these things as close as possible to their essences.[8] Also, in everything of which philosophy gives an account that is demonstrative and certain, religion gives an account based on persuasive arguments. Finally, philosophy is prior to religion in time.

56   Again, it is evident that when one seeks to bring into actual existence the intelligibles of the things depending on the will supplied by practical philosophy,[1] he ought to prescribe the conditions that render possible their actual existence.[2] Once the **15** conditions that render their actual existence possible are prescribed, the voluntary intelligibles are embodied in laws.[3] Therefore the legislator is he who, by the excellence of his deliberation, has the capacity to find the conditions required for the actual existence of voluntary intelligibles in such a way as to lead to the achievement of supreme happiness. It is also evident that only after perceiving them by his intellect should the legislator seek to discover their conditions, and he cannot find their conditions that **42** enable him to guide others toward supreme happiness without having perceived supreme happiness with his intellect.[4] Nor can these things become intelligible (and the legislative craft thereby hold the supreme office) without his having beforehand acquired

philosophy. Therefore, if he intends to possess a craft that is authoritative rather than subservient, the legislator must be a   5 philosopher. Similarly, if the philosopher who has acquired the theoretical virtues does not have the capacity for bringing them about in all others according to their capacities, then what he has acquired from them has no validity. Yet he cannot find the states and the conditions by which the voluntary intelligibles assume actual existence,[5] if he does not possess the deliberative virtue; and the deliberative virtue cannot exist in him without the practical[6] virtue. Moreover, he cannot bring them about in all others accord-   10 ing to their capacities except by a faculty that enables him to excel in persuasion and in representing things through images.

57   It follows, then, that the idea of *Imam,* Philosopher, and Legislator is a single idea.[1] However, the name *philosopher* signi- fies primarily theoretical virtue. But if it be determined that the theoretical virtue reach its ultimate perfection in every respect, it follows necessarily that he must possess all the other faculties as well.[2] *Legislator* signifies excellence of knowledge concerning   15 the conditions of practical[3] intelligibles, the faculty for finding them, and the faculty for bringing them about in nations and cities. When it is determined that they be brought into existence on the basis of knowledge, it will follow that the theoretical virtue must precede the others—the existence of the inferior presupposes the existence of the higher.[4] The name *prince* signifies sovereignty and ability. To be completely able, one has to possess the power of   **43** the greatest ability. His ability to do a thing must not result only from external things; he himself must possess great ability because his art, skill, and virtue are of exceedingly great power. This is not possible except by great power of knowledge, great power of deliberation, and great power of [moral] virtue and art. Otherwise he is not truly able nor sovereign. For if his ability stops short of   5 this, it is still imperfect. Similarly, if his ability is restricted to goods inferior to supreme happiness, his ability is incomplete and he is not perfect. Therefore the true prince is the same as the philosopher-legislator. As to the idea of *Imam* in the Arabic lan- guage, it signifies merely the one whose example is followed and who is well received: that is, either his perfection is well received   10 or his purpose is well received. If he is not well received in all the

infinite activities, virtues, and arts, then he is not truly well received. Only when all other arts, virtues, and activities seek to realize *his* purpose and no other, will his art be the most powerful art, his [moral] virtue the most powerful virtue, his deliberation the most powerful deliberation, and his science the most powerful science. For with all of these powers he will be exploiting the   15 powers of others so as to accomplish his own purpose.[5] This is not possible without the theoretical sciences, without the greatest of all deliberative virtues, and without the rest of those things that are in the philosopher.[6]

58   So let it be clear to you that the idea of the Philosopher, Supreme Ruler, Prince, Legislator, and *Imam* is but a single idea. No matter which one of these words[1] you take, if you proceed to look at what each of them signifies among the majority of those   **44** who speak our language, you will find that they all finally agree by signifying one and the same idea.

59   Once the images representing the theoretical things[1] demonstrated in the theoretical sciences are produced in the souls of the multitude and they are made to assent to their images, and once the practical[2] things (together with the conditions of the possibility of their existence) take hold of their souls and dominate   5 them so that they are unable to resolve to do anything else, then the theoretical and practical things are realized. Now these things are *philosophy* when they are in the soul of the legislator. They are *religion* when they are in the souls of the multitude. For when the legislator knows these things, they are evident to him by sure insight, whereas what is established in the souls of the multitude is through an image and a persuasive argument. Although it is the legislator who also represents these things through images,   10 neither the images nor the persuasive arguments are intended for himself. As far as he is concerned, they are certain. He is the one who invents the images and the persuasive arguments, but not for the sake of establishing these things in his own soul as a religion for himself. No, the images and the persuasive arguments are intended for others, whereas, so far as he is concerned, these things are certain. They are a religion for others, whereas, so far as he is concerned, they are philosophy.[3] Such, then, is true philosophy and the true philosopher.

60   As for mutilated philosophy: the counterfeit philosopher, the vain philosopher, or the false philosopher is the one who sets   15 out to study the theoretical sciences without being prepared for them. For he who sets out to inquire ought to be innately equipped for the theoretical sciences—that is, fulfill the conditions prescribed by Plato in the *Republic*:[1] he should excel in comprehending and conceiving that which is essential. Moreover, he should have good memory and be able to endure the toil of study. He should love truthfulness and truthful people, and justice and just people; and   **45** not be headstrong or a wrangler about what he desires. He should not be gluttonous for food and drink, and should by natural disposition disdain the appetites, the *dirhem,* the *dinar,* and the like. He should be high-minded and avoid what is considered disgraceful. He should be pious, yield easily to goodness and justice, and be stubborn in yielding to evil and injustice. And he should be strongly determined in favor of the right thing. Moreover, he   5 should be brought up according to laws and habits that resemble his innate disposition. He should have sound conviction about the opinions of the religion in which he is reared, hold fast to the virtuous acts in his religion, and not forsake all or most of them. Furthermore, he should hold fast to the generally accepted virtues and not forsake the generally accepted noble acts.[2] For if a youth is such, and then sets out to study philosophy and learns it, it is   10 possible that he will not become a counterfeit or a vain or a false philosopher.

61   The false philosopher is he who acquires the theoretical sciences without achieving the utmost perfection so as to be able to introduce others to what he knows insofar as their capacity permits. The vain philosopher is he who learns the theoretical sciences, but without going any further and without being habituated to doing the acts considered virtuous by a certain religion or the   15 generally accepted noble acts. Instead he follows his own inclination and appetites in everything, whatever they may happen to be. The counterfeit philosopher is he who studies the theoretical sciences without being naturally equipped for them. Therefore, although the counterfeit and the vain may complete the study of the theoretical sciences, in the end their possession of them diminishes little by little. By the time they reach the age at which a man   **46**

should become perfect in the virtues, their knowledge will have been completely extinguished, even more so than the extinction of the fire [sun] of Heraclitus mentioned by Plato.[1] For the natural dispositions of the former and the habit of the latter overpower what they might have remembered in their youth and make it burdensome for them to retain what they had patiently toiled for. They neglect it, and what they retain begins to diminish little by little until its fire becomes ineffective and extinguished, and they 5 gather no fruit from it. As for the false philosopher, he is the one who is not yet aware of the purpose for which philosophy is pursued. He acquires the theoretical sciences, or only some portion thereof, and holds the opinion that the purpose of the measure he has acquired consists in certain kinds of happiness that are believed to be so or are considered by the multitude to be good things. Therefore he rests there to enjoy that happiness, aspiring to achieve this purpose with his knowledge. He may achieve his 10 purpose and settle for it, or else find his purpose difficult to achieve and so hold the opinion that the knowledge he has is superfluous. Such is the false philosopher.

62   The true philosopher is the one mentioned before.[1] If after reaching this stage no use is made of him, the fact that he is of no use to others is not his fault but the fault of those who either do not listen or are not of the opinion that they should listen to him.[2] Therefore the prince or the *imam* is prince and 15 *imam* by virtue of his skill and art, regardless of whether or not anyone acknowledges him, whether or not he is obeyed, whether or not he is supported in his purpose by any group; just as the physician is physician by virtue of his skill and his ability to heal the sick, whether or not there are sick men for him to heal, whether or not he finds tools to use in his activity, whether he is prosperous or poor—not having any of these things does not do away with his physicianship. Similarly, neither the *imamate* of the *imam,* the 47 philosophy of the philosopher, nor the princeship of the prince is done away with by his not having tools to use in his activities or men to employ in reaching his purpose.[3]

63   The philosophy that answers to this description was handed down to us by the Greeks from Plato and Aristotle only. Both have given us an account of philosophy, but not without

giving us also an account of the ways to it and of the ways to   5
re-establish it when it becomes confused or extinct. We shall begin
by expounding first the philosophy of Plato and the ranks of
order of his philosophy. We shall begin with the first part of the
philosophy of Plato, and then order one part of his philosophy
after another until we reach its end. We shall do the same with the
philosophy presented to us by Aristotle, beginning with the first
part of his philosophy.

64   So let it be clear to you that, in what they presented, their
purpose[1] is the same, and that they intended to offer one and the   10
same philosophy.

Philosophy of Plato and Aristotle
Part II
The Philosophy of Plato

THE PHILOSOPHY OF PLATO,

ITS PARTS, THE RANKS OF ORDER

OF ITS PARTS, FROM THE BEGINNING

TO THE END

i

1   First he investigated the human things that make man enviable as to which of them constitutes the perfection of man as man, for every being has a perfection. Thus he investigated whether man's perfection consists only in his having his bodily organs unimpaired, a beautiful face, and soft skin; or whether it consists also in his having a distinguished ancestry and tribe, or having a   5 large tribe and many friends and lovers; or whether it consists also in his being prosperous; or being glorified and exalted, ruling over a group or a city in which his command is enforced and which submits to his wish. In order to attain the happiness that gives him his ultimate perfection, is it sufficient for man to have some or all of these? It became evident to him as he investigated these things that either they are themselves not happiness at all   10 but are only believed to be happiness, or they are not themselves sufficient for man to attain happiness without having something else in addition to them or to some of them.

2   Then he investigated what this other thing must be. It became evident to him that this other thing, whose attainment is the attainment of happiness, is a certain knowledge and a certain way of life.

All this is to be found in his book called the *Alcibiades* (that   15
is to say,[1] *model*) *Major,* which is known as *On Man.*

3   Then, after that, he investigated what this knowledge is   **4**
and its distinguishing mark, until he found what it is, its distinguishing mark, its character, and that it is knowledge of the
substance of each of the beings: this knowledge is the final perfection of man and the highest perfection he can possess.[1] This is to
be found in his book that he called the *Theaetetus* (meaning *vol-*   5
untary).

4   Then, after that, he investigated the happiness that is truly
happiness, what it is, from which kind of knowledge it proceeds,
which state of character it is, and which act it is. He distinguished
it from what is believed to be happiness but is not. And he made
it known that the virtuous way of life is what leads to the achievement of this happiness. That is to be found in his book that he
called the *Philebus* (meaning *beloved*).   10

ii

5   When he had recognized the knowledge and the way of life
that make man happy and perfect, he first began to investigate the
knowledge: if man should aspire to a knowledge of the beings that
has this character, can he attain it? Or is it the case—as Protagoras
(*the carrier*[1] *of bricks*) asserts—that man cannot attain such   15
knowledge of the beings, that this is not the knowledge that is possible and that man is naturally capable of attaining, that the
knowledge he attains about the beings is rather the opinion of each   5
of those who speculate about things and the conviction each happens to hold, and that the knowledge natural to man is relative
to the conviction formed by each individual and is not this other
knowledge that one may aspire to but will not reach? After investigating Protagoras' argument, Plato explained that, contrary to   5
what Protagoras asserts, this knowledge, whose character was
explained in the *Theaetetus,* can be attained and does exist,[2] and
that this is the knowledge that belongs to human perfection, not the
one asserted by Protagoras. This is to be found in his book known
as the *Protagoras.*[3]

6 Then he investigated whether this attainable knowledge
is attained by chance or by investigation or by instruction and   10
study; and whether a way of investigation or instruction or study
exists by which to attain this knowledge, or whether no way of
investigation, instruction, or study by which to attain this knowledge exists at all—as Meno (meaning *fixed*) used to assert. For
he [Meno] claimed that investigation and instruction and study are
futile, useless, and do not lead to knowledge; that man either   15
knows a thing, not through investigation or instruction or study,
but by nature and chance, or does not know it; what is[1] not known
cannot become known either by investigation or by study or by
inference; and the unknown remains unknown forever, despite
what the protagonists of investigation assert about a thing's being
apprehended by investigation, instruction, or study. It became   6
clear to him [Plato] that this knowledge *can* be attained by investigation and by a faculty and art according to which that investigation proceeds. This is to be found in his book known as the *Meno*.

iii

7 When it had become evident to him that, of all the sciences,
it is by this science that the perfection of man ought to be attained, that there is here an art and a faculty with which the
beings can be investigated to the point of achieving this knowl-   5
edge, and that there is here an investigation, study, or instruction
that is a way to this knowledge—then he proceeded to find out
which art supplies this knowledge and by which investigation it
is attained. He set about canvassing the generally accepted arts and
generally accepted investigations: that is, generally accepted among
the citizens of cities and nations.

First, he began to investigate whether religious[1] speculation   10
and the religious investigation of the beings supply this knowledge
and that desired way of life; and whether the religious syllogistic
art that conducts this kind of investigation of the beings and the
ways of life supplies this knowledge, or does not supply it at all,
or is not adequate for supplying this knowledge of the beings and
this way of life. It became clear to him, further, how much knowl-   15

edge of the beings and knowledge of the ways of life is supplied by religious investigation and the religious syllogistic art, and that the amount they supply is not sufficient. All this is to be found in the *Euthyphron* (the name of a man)—*On Piety*.

8 Then, after that, he investigated whether that art is the science of language, and whether when man comprehends the *significative names*[1] and the ideas they signify according to the multitude of the nation that speaks the language in question, and investigates and knows them according to the method of the students of the science of language, he will have a comprehensive knowledge of the substances[2] of things and attain that desired knowledge about them; for the students of this art themselves believe so. It became evident to him that this art does not supply that knowledge at all, and he explained how much[3] it supplies of the knowledge that can provide a *way* to that knowledge. This is to be found in his book known as the *Cratylus*.

9 Then, since the former arts do not supply this knowledge, he investigated whether the art that supplies it is poetry; whether the faculty for obtaining this knowledge of the beings is the ability to compose poems and the ability to acquire that of which poems and poetic statements are made; whether or not the recitation of poems, the understanding of their meanings, and the maxims they contain, supply us with that knowledge of the natural beings and knowledge of the desired way of life; whether or not to form one's character by poems and improve oneself by means of the maxims they contain is sufficient for man to make him lead the perfect human way of life; and whether or not the investigation of the beings and the ways of life by the poetic method is the way to that knowledge and that way of life. It became evident to him, further, how much knowledge is supplied by poetry and what the value of poetry is for being human. He explained that the generally accepted poetic method does not ever supply any of this at all, but that it leads one far away from it. That is to be found in his book known as the *Ion*.

10 Then he made a similar investigation of the art of rhetoric: whether rhetoric, or the use of rhetorical opinion when inquiring into the beings, supplies us with that knowledge about them or supplies us with knowledge of that way of life. He ex-

7

5

10

15

20

8

plained that it does not do so. It became evident to him, further, how much knowledge is supplied by rhetoric and what is the value of the amount it supplies.[1] That is to be found in his book   5
known as the *Gorgias* (meaning *service*).

11   Then he made a similar[1] investigation of the art of sophistry and whether or not sophistry is the inquiry that supplies the desired knowledge. He explained that sophistry does not supply that knowledge and that sophistical inquiry is not the way to that   10
knowledge. He explained, further, the value of sophistry. That is to be found in the *Sophist* (*falsifier*) and in the *Euthydemus* (a man). For in his book known as the *Sophist* he made known what the art of sophistry is, what it does, and how many aims it pursues; what is the sophistical man, how many kinds of him there are, and into what sort of affairs he inquires; and that[2] he does not conduct the investigation that leads man to the desired   15
knowledge and does not inquire at all into matters subject to knowledge. As for the *Euthydemus,* he explained in it the manner of sophistical inquiry and sophistical teaching, how it comes pretty close to being play, and how it does not supply that knowledge or   9
lead to a knowledge useful either in theory or in practice.

12   Then, after that, he inquired into the investigations[1] of the dialecticians and into the dialectical investigation, whether or not it leads man to that knowledge, and whether or not it is adequate for supplying it. He explained that it is extremely valuable   5
for arriving at that knowledge; indeed, frequently it is impossible to come to that knowledge until the thing is investigated dialectically. It does not supply that knowledge from the outset, however. No, in order to attain that knowledge, another faculty is needed along with, and in addition to, the faculty for dialectical exercise. That is to be found in his book known as the *Parmenides* (meaning   10
compassion).

iv

13   When he had exhausted all the generally accepted scientific or theoretical arts and found that none of them supplies this knowledge of the beings or that way of life, he began next to

investigate the practical arts and the actions originating in these arts: whether, when man encompasses all the [practical] arts or the amount of knowledge they contain, he will have attained that   15
knowledge of all the beings; and whether or not the actions offered by these arts supply that desired way of life, for these arts combine knowledge and action. Therefore he investigated whether the sciences supplied by these arts constitute that knowledge and whether the actions originating in them constitute that way of life.   10
He explained that they do not supply that knowledge or constitute that way of life, and that[1] the intention of those who acquire them is not ultimate perfection, but rather[2] to obtain by them only useful and gainful things. Now the useful may be necessary, while the gainful is always good[3] but not necessary. With what they acquire   5
of these arts, they intend, then, either necessary things or gain, that is, what is good.

V

14   Therefore, when these two [that is, the useful and the gainful] had come to light in relation to all the practical arts, he began to investigate what the necessary is and what the gainful is. (There is no difference between investigating gain, what is gainful, and what is good, for these are almost synonyms referring to the   10
same idea.) He investigated the things that are good in the eyes of the multitude and the things that are gainful in the eyes of the multitude, whether they are truly good and gainful. He also investigated whether the things that are useful in the eyes of the multitude are truly as they believe them to be or not. He explained that they are not, and here he went through all the things that are good gains in the eyes of the multitude.   15
This is to be found in his book known as *Alcibiades Minor*.

15   Then, after that, he investigated the truly useful things, the truly gainful things, and the gains that are truly good, and how one does not come to any of them by way of the generally accepted arts.

16   Then he explained the relation of the things useful and gainful in the eyes of the multitude to the things truly useful and

gainful, how [true] gains and the goods are nothing but that knowl-   20
edge and that desired way of life, and how the practical arts are   11
not adequate for obtaining the gain that is the true gain.

That is to be found in his book that he called the *Hipparchus*
(*observation*).

17   Then he investigated whether that desired perfection and
desired end are obtained by the way of life of the hypocrites and   5
those who falsify their purposes before people by feigning nobility
and hiding another end. For this is the way of life in which the
multitude saw strength and fortitude and for which they would
envy a man. Hence he also investigated whether this way of life
is what the multitude believes it to be. That is to be found in two of
his books, which he named after two *men*[1] who were extreme
hypocrites and extremely false in their ways of life and in their   10
actions and who were considered sophists. Having reached the
limit in quarrelsomeness and sophistical persuasion about themselves in speech and deed, they were reputed for their strength and
fortitude. These are the two books, the first of which he called
Hippias the [Major] Sophist[2] and the other, *Hippias the [Minor]
Sophist.*[3] He explained regarding this way of life, too, that it does
not supply the desired end but leads far away from it.   15

18   Then he investigated the pleasure-seekers' way of life   12
and whether or not it is a way of life by which man achieves the
desired perfection. He explained the pleasure that is true pleasure;
what the pleasure is that is generally accepted and desired by the
multitude; that true pleasure is the pleasure originating in the
desired perfection; and that no part of the pleasure-seekers' way of   5
life leads to the pleasure originating in the desired perfection. This
is to be found in his book *On Pleasure [Symposium],*[1] which is
attributed to Socrates.

vi

19   When it had become evident to him that none of the arts
practiced by the multitude is a scientific art that supplies that
knowledge, a practical art that supplies that knowledge, or a practical art that supplies that way of life, and that none of the ways of

life generally accepted among them leads to happiness, he himself   10
had to present and explain how the theoretical art that supplies
that knowledge of the beings ought to be and how the practical art
that supplies man with that desired way of life ought to be. He
explained in his book known as the *Theages* (that is to say,
experience) what that theoretical art is, and that it is philosophy.
He explained who the man is who gives an account of that knowl-   15
edge, and that he is the philosopher. And he explained what the
idea of the Philosopher is and what his activity is.

20   Then he explained in his book known as the ›*Erastai*   **13**
[*Lovers*][1] that philosophy is not merely a good thing; no, it is that
which is truly useful. Moreover, it is not useful although unneces-
sary, but both useful and necessary for being human.

21   Then, after that, he investigated the practical art that
supplies that desired way of life, orders the actions, and guides   5
souls toward happiness. He explained that it is the princely and
political art. And he explained the idea of the Prince and the
Statesman.[1]

22   Then he explained that the man who is philosopher and
the man who is prince are the same; each of them is rendered
perfect by a single skill and a single faculty;[1] each of them possesses a single skill that supplies the desired knowledge and the
desired way of life from the outset;[2] and each of the two[3] [skills   10
or faculties] is the agent producing that happiness which is true
happiness in those who have acquired it and in all others.

23   Then he investigated what moderation is. He investigated
the moderation generally accepted in cities; what the moderation
is that is true moderation; what the moderate man is who is believed to be moderate; what the moderate man is who is truly
moderate; what is the way of life of those who are truly moderate;   15
and how the multitude have been ignorant of what true moderation
is. That is to be found in his book known as the *Charmides*.

Similarly, he investigated the courage because of which the
citizens of cities are reputed for being courageous. He explained
what the courage is that is believed by the multitude to be courage,
and he explained the courage that is true courage. That is to be
found in his book called the *Laches* (meaning *preparation*).   20

24   Then he investigated love and friendship. He investigated   **14**

that which is friendship in the eyes of the multitude and that which
is true friendship and love, and that which is truly lovable and
that which is lovable in the eyes of the multitude.[1]

25   Then he closely investigated how the man who is resolved
to become a philosopher or a statesman and achieve something   5
good ought to be, and how he ought to be possessed by what he
seeks, not think of anything else, and revel in it. Since revelling
in this thing and seduction by it are subsumed under the genus of
rapture, he therefore investigated what rapture is and its genus.
Since some revelling and seduction are blamable and some praiseworthy, and since some praiseworthy things are believed by the   10
multitude to be praiseworthy although they may not be truly
praiseworthy, while others are truly praiseworthy, he investigated
both of them. And since the excess of seduction and revelling is
attributed to enchantment and madness, and upon the first view
these are believed to be blamable, he investigated also the enchantment and madness that are said to be blamable. He mentioned that   15
the ones who bestow blame upon these two do praise them sometimes. For they believe that, frequently, men become enchanted
and mad from divine causes, so much so that some of them foretell
future events, and others are possessed by the love of goodness and
the quest of the virtues practiced in mosques and temples. Others
associate the poets who are skilful in making poems with spirits   **15**
as the cause of their enchantment and madness. These and similar
things belong to praiseworthy enchantment and madness. He investigated the praiseworthy seduction, revelling, rapture, enchantment, and madness, when it is divine, in what manner it occurs,
in which soul it occurs, and in which man it occurs. He mentioned   5
that he who praises this [madness and so on] is convinced that it
occurs in the man whose soul is divine: that is, the man who craves
and longs for divine things. He began to investigate the character
of this soul; and how some revelling, seduction, rapture, madness,
and enchantment is praiseworthy and divine, while some is blame-
worthy and human. As to that which is human, human madness is
frequently associated with bestial madness, so that there are those 10
whose madness is that of a lion and their enchantment that of a
bull, and those whose madness and enchantment are those of a he-
goat. He investigated all of these things, distinguished bestial

revelling from revelling in divine things, and investigated the kinds of enchantment and revelling in virtuous things, which are associated with divine causes. And he explained that philosophy, statesmanship, and perfection cannot be achieved unless the soul of the man who seeks them revels in them and in the end that he[1]   15 seeks; neither the philosopher nor the statesman can perform his activity with which he seeks the virtuous end unless that very revelling continues to be in him.

26   Then he investigated the methods that the man who aims at philosophy should use in his investigation. He mentioned   **16** that they are the method of division and the method of bringing together.[1]

27   Then he investigated the method of instruction: how it is conducted by two methods—the method of rhetoric and another method he called *dialectic*; and how both of these methods can be employed in conversation and in speaking and employed in writing.

28   Then he explained the value of conversation and the value of writing, the extent to which instruction through writing is defec-   5 tive when compared to conversation, and what it is that writing achieves and the extent to which conversation fails in this respect; and how the superior method of instruction is conversation, while the method of writing is inferior.[1] He explained what things a man ought to know in order to become a philosopher.

All this is to be found in a book of his that he called the *Phaedrus* (the meaning of this word in Arabic is *shining* or *illuminating*).   10

vii

29   When it had become evident to him that this art is not one of the generally accepted arts, nor is this way of life, which is truly a virtuous way of life, generally accepted among nations and cities, and that neither the perfect philosopher nor the perfect prince could use his acts in the nations and cities that existed in his time, nor could the reveller who is in search of the two [perfections] and of the virtuous way of life either study or investigate them   15

in such cities and nations, he then began to investigate whether
when these [perfections] become too difficult to find, one ought
to settle for the opinions he finds among his ancestors or among
the citizens of his city,[1] and whether he should settle for the ways
of life he finds among the citizens of his city or nation. He explained   **17**
that one ought not to settle for them without investigating them and
without seeking to arrive at the virtuous things that are truly
virtuous,[2] whether these are the same as the opinions and the ways
of life of the citizens of his city or opposed to them; and he ought
to seek the truth among the opinions, and among the ways of life
seek the virtuous one that is truly virtuous. This is to be found in   **5**
his book that he called the *Crito*; it is also called the *Apology of
Socrates*.[3]

   30   Then he investigated in another book of his whether man
ought or ought not to prefer security and life along with ignorance,
a base way of life, and bad actions—whether there is or is not a
difference between man's existence and life when leading such a   **10**
way of life, and his existence and life, not as a man, but as a beast
and worse than a beast. Whether there is a difference between
man's death and nonexistence, his existence when combined with
ignorance and the leading of this base way of life, and his being a
beast and worse than a beast. Whether it is preferable to lead a
beast's way of life and a way of life worse than a beast's way of
life, or to die. Whether, when man despairs of existing for the rest   **15**
of his days in conformity with the virtuous way of life and with
philosophy, and knows that to the end of his days his existence will
depend on leading a bestial way of life or a way of life by which
he becomes worse than a beast, he ought to lead such an existence
and prefer it, or he ought to view death as preferable. And
whether, when he needs to be moderate or courageous or to possess
any other virtue, and neither this virtue, this moderation, nor this   **20**
courage is true virtue or moderation or courage but only believed
to be so, man ought to prefer life, or he ought to prefer
death. He investigated these things in two of his books; the first   **18**
is the *Protest of Socrates Against the Athenians*,[1] and the second
is his book known as the *Phaedo*.[2]

   He explained[3] that one ought to prefer death to such a life and

that such a life only leads him to one of two conditions: the performance of either bestial activities alone or else activities worse   5
than bestial. For there is no difference between [seeing] a man
who possesses the most perfect bestiality and performs the most
perfect activities thereof, and assuming that he is dead and transformed into that beast and its shape. Thus there is no difference
between a man who acts like a fish,[4] and a fish with a shape[5] like
that of a man: *his*[6] only virtue is his[7] human shape and the fact   10
that he acts like a *perfect* fish. Nor is there any difference between
this and his shape's being like a fish, his acting like a fish, and yet
calculating his actions well like a man. For in all this he does not
possess humanity except insofar as the calculation, by which he
performs the activity of that beast well, is the calculation of a man.
He [Plato] explained that the more perfectly one performs the
activity of the beast, the further he is from being human; had the   15
activities of that beast proceeded from some animate body having
the shape of that beast along with man's calculation about these   **19**
activities, such activities would be nothing but the most perfect
activity that can proceed from that beast—the more perfectly and
effectively the animate body performs the activities of that beast,
the further it is from being human.

Therefore he saw that the time and life of whoever does not
investigate are not those of a human being, and that he should
not mind dying and[8] preferring death to life as Socrates did. For   5
when he [Socrates] knew that he could not survive except by conforming to false opinions and leading a base way of life, he
preferred death to life. This made it evident that if man shares in
[the opinions and the ways of life of] the citizens of those nations
and cities, or those who resemble them, his life will not be that
of a human being; and if he should wish to depart from their ways
and become isolated from them and seek to achieve perfection, he   10
will lead a poor existence. It is very unlikely[9] that he could
achieve what he wants. For he will necessarily be visited by one
of two fates, either death or deprivation of perfection.

Therefore[10] it became evident that one needs another city and
another nation, different from the cities and nations existing at
that time. Therefore he had to investigate what distinguishes *that*

city. He started by investigating what true justice is,[11] how it   15
ought to be, and how it ought to be applied. As he was conducting this investigation, he found he had to investigate the justice   **20**
generally accepted and applied in cities.

viii

31   When he had investigated it and looked around him, it
became evident to him that it is complete injustice and extreme
evil; these grave evils—and they are extremely grave—would not
slacken or vanish so long as the cities continued as they were;
another city ought to be founded which is different from those   5
cities, in which and in the like of which there would be true justice
and all the goods that are truly good. This will be a city that will
not lack anything that leads its citizens to happiness. Now if it
should be decided that this city will have *all* the things by means
of which happiness is achieved, it is indispensable for its inhabitants
that the princely craft in it be true philosophy, that philosophers   10
constitute its highest part, and that those who hold other ranks be
subordinate to them.
32   Then he mentioned next the cities antagonistic[1] to it and
the way of life of each; and he stated the causes of the changes
that inhere in virtuous cities so that they change and are turned
into the opposite cities. For it is indeed in this city alone that man
arrives at the desired perfection.
This is to be found in his book the *Republic*.[2]

ix

33   When this city had been rendered perfect in speech, he   15
next presented in the *Timaeus* an account of the divine and natural
beings[1] as they are perceived by the intellect and known by means
of that science; [he showed] what distinguishes the sciences that
ought to be set up in that city; how everything that is not yet
known will be inquired into and a comprehensive investigation of

it will be made in that city; and how there will be a succession of
men who will investigate this science and preserve what is dis-
covered of it, until all of it is found.[2]   20

34   Then he presented in the *Laws* the virtuous ways[1] of life   **21**
that the inhabitants of this city should be made to follow.

35   Then he explained what distinguishes the human perfection achieved by him who combines the theoretical sciences and the
political and practical sciences, and what ought to be his rank   5
in this city. He explained that it is the rank of ruling the city.
This is to be found in his book known as the *Critias* (meaning
separating out the truths), where Plato narrates how Critias described how the one generated by Timaeus and whom Socrates
reared and educated ought to be—meaning by this the one who
combines the capacity for the knowledge and the art of each of the 10
two, which are presented in the *Timaeus* and in the *Laws*.

There remained for him now to have this city realized in deed.
He mentioned that this is accomplished only by the legislator
of this city. Therefore he afterwards investigated how the legislator ought to be. That is to be found in his book that he called
the *Epinomis* (meaning *investigator*).

x

36   When he had done this, he afterwards investigated the   15
manner and the method by means of which the citizens of cities
and nations ought to be instructed in this science and their character formed by those ways of life, whether the method ought to be
the one used by Socrates or the one that was the method of Thrasy- **22**
machus. Here he delineated once again Socrates' method for
realizing his aim of making his own people understand through
scientific investigation the ignorance they were in. He explained
Thrasymachus' method and made it known that Thrasymachus
was more able than Socrates to form the character of the youth
and instruct the multitude; Socrates possessed only the ability to   5
conduct a scientific investigation of justice and the virtues,[1] and
a power of love, but did not possess the ability to form the character of the youth and the multitude;[2] and the philosopher, the

prince, and the legislator ought to be able to use both methods: the Socratic method with the elect, and Thrasymachus' method with the youth and the multitude.[3]

37 Then, after that, he investigated what orders of rank the princes, the philosophers, and the virtuous ought to have in the eyes of the citizens of the city, by what means the citizens of the city ought to glorify them, and by what means the virtuous ought to be exalted and the princes exalted. That is to be found in a book he called the *Menexenus*. He stated that his predecessors had overlooked this.

38 Then, after that, he mentioned once again the multitude of the citizens of cities and nations living in his time. He stated that the perfect man, the man who investigates, and the virtuous man are in grave danger in their midst; one ought to devise a plan for moving them [the multitude] away from their ways of life and opinions to truth and to the virtuous ways of life, or closer to them. In some *Letters* he composed he gave an account of how to abolish the ways of life of nations and the corrupt laws that prevail in the cities, how to move the cities and nations away from them, and how to reform their ways of life. He described in these letters his own view as to the mode of government that ought to be applied in order to move them gradually to virtuous ways of life and to correct laws. As an example of this, he mentioned the Athenians (his own people) and their ways of life. He described how to abolish their laws and how to turn them away from them. He described his view regarding the way in which they could be moved gradually, and he described the opinions and the laws toward which they should be moved after the abolition of their ways of life and laws.

This, then, is where the philosophy of Plato terminated.

Philosophy of Plato and Aristotle

Part III

The Philosophy of Aristotle

THE PHILOSOPHY OF ARISTOTLE,

THE PARTS OF HIS PHILOSOPHY,

THE RANKS OF ORDER OF ITS PARTS,

THE POSITION FROM WHICH HE

STARTED AND THE ONE HE REACHED

i

1   Aristotle sees the perfection of man as Plato sees it and   5
more.[1] However, because man's perfection is not self-evident or
easy to explain by a demonstration leading to certainty, he saw fit
to start from a position anterior to that from which Plato had
started.[2] He saw four things that everyone pursues from the outset
and considers desirable and good—they are desired and pursued
by nature, as it were, from the beginning, and no other pursuit   10
precedes them in time: (1) the soundness of the human body, (2)
the soundness of the senses, (3) the soundness of the capacity for
knowing how to discern what leads to the soundness of the body
and the senses, and (4) the soundness of the power to labor at
what leads to their soundness.[3] This (3) is the kind of knowledge
that is useful and necessary. And this (4) is the kind of labor
that is useful, necessary, and preferred to everything else, be it
the labor of a man by himself, or accompanied by the labor of   15
others for him, or accompanied by his labor for others, and whether
he performs it by deed or speech. The deed by which this labor
is performed is the useful and necessary deed that has priority,

and the speech by which this labor is performed is the useful and necessary speech. Beyond this, one may prefer also that these four things exist in the most excellent state of their soundness.[4]

2 Then he found out that next to desiring these four, the **60** soul desires to understand the causes of sensible things, of what is observed in the heaven and on earth, and of what man sees in his own soul and the state in which he finds it. He desires to know the truth of what insinuates itself into souls and comes to the mind, be it a thing that insinuates itself into a man's own soul or something that has insinuated itself into the soul of someone else who **5** has informed him of it. Now such things do not belong to any of those four; knowledge of them is not useful for the soundness of any of the four or with regard to anything else or for the sake of anything else, apart from knowing the thing and resting upon the knowledge of it. Yet when man understands any of them he finds it pleasant and delights in it. The firmer and nearer to certainty his knowledge, the greater his rejoicing and his pleasure in what he understands.[1] The more perfect the being he apprehends and understands, the greater his rejoicing and his pleasure with his **10** apprehension.

Subsequently man comes to the view that he possesses, because of this apprehension, a certain excellence, nobility, high rank, and exalted position, although other men do not acknowledge this. No, as a result of his own reflection he sees himself to have attained excellence and perfection, even though others do not perceive it. He considers himself exalted and of a high rank, and marvels at himself and at what he has apprehended. Then he comes to the view that perhaps this ought to be acknowledged by men, or to the view that he ought to be honored, magnified, glorified, **15** and eulogized by others for it, especially with regard to such things as are not likely to be known by everyone and are difficult for all to apprehend.[2]

Although all men view such knowledge and cognitions as neither necessary nor useful for any of those four things, but rather beyond the necessary and the useful, they view them nevertheless as something exalted and of a high rank. Therefore, from the outset, they divide the knowledge desired by man into two **20** kinds: a knowledge desired for its use for the soundness of those

four things or for the most excellent state of their soundness, and
a knowledge that is beyond the merely useful knowledge and that
is desired for itself and not for anything else. This division derives
its validity from the soul's desire for the two kinds of knowledge,
even before deciding between them as to which is to be preferred   **61**
and which to be avoided. Consequently, he called the first kind
practical, and the second kind *theoretical,* science.[3]

Moreover, although men may use their *senses* to discern what
is useful to them in those four pursuits, they may use them also
to apprehend and know what is not useful to them in any one of   5
those pursuits. They desire sensible things, the apprehension of
which by sense-perception is not useful for any of those four
things—for instance, statues, elegant sceneries, objects delightful
to hear and to smell, and objects pleasurable to touch—for
nothing else besides having them as pleasurable objects of sense-
perception. For "pleasurable" means nothing other than that one
is apprehending most excellently a most excellent object of
apprehension; for there cannot be pleasure without apprehension;
it is present in [animals] that apprehend by sense-perception and   10
absent from those that do not.[4] Likewise, there are, besides the
knowledge of sensible things, other cognitions obtained by sense-
perception that man may desire although he confines himself to
knowing and apprehending and to the pleasure he experiences in
apprehending them: for instance, the myths, stories, histories of
peoples, and histories of nations, that man narrates and to which
he listens solely for the delight they give. (For to delight in some-   15
thing means nothing other than the achievement of comfort and
pleasure.) Likewise, looking at imitators and listening to imitative
statements, listening to poems, and going over what one comprehends of the poems and the myths he recites or reads, are used
by the man who delights in them and is comforted by them only for
his pleasure in what he comprehends.[5] The more certain his   20
apprehension, the more perfect his pleasure. The more excellent
and perfect in himself the man who comprehends, the more perfect
and complete his pleasure in his apprehension. Therefore these,
too, are cognitions and apprehensions that are sought only for
the sake of apprehension and the pleasure of apprehension, not
for the sake of being utilized with respect to those four things.

And although men may use them on the ground that they are   **62**
also useful with respect to those four, it is only accidentally that
he who intends pleasure uses them for the sake of any of those four.

3 Then he found out that there are, in addition to what is
apprehended by the senses, certain among the necessary cognitions
that originate with man as it were innately and by nature. Frequently   5
man uses the cognitions, acquired by the senses, in his labor for
the soundness of those four things; then he finds out that the cognitions gained by the senses are insufficient; so he turns and uses
the innate cognitions originating in him. Yet when he applies himself to the satisfaction of all his needs, he sees that the cognitions
originating in him are also insufficient for many things most of   10
the time, and finds that they do not embrace all his needs. Consequently, he hesitates about many of his needs and does not act
upon them until he considers, thinks, investigates, and deliberates.
Usually he attempts to obtain this knowledge from others: he
asks and consults with them about what he does not think he can
infer and discover fully by himself. All this is because he is not
innately directed to such knowledge. Through investigation, con-   15
sideration, deliberation, and reasoning, he uncovers a knowledge
he did not have originally. But frequently he is perplexed and
unable to determine which of two alternatives is useful and which
harmful; or perhaps it becomes obvious to him after investigation
that he has made a mistake in many of his inferences without being
aware of it at first. It is also characteristic of the sciences he
acquires through his desire for them, his investigation of them,
and his deliberation upon them, that some are firmer and some
shakier than others. However, once he attains *certainty* about what   20
he was investigating, this is the perfect science of what he wants to
know and the end beyond which he can hope for no better assurance and reliability. This, then, is man's situation with respect to
the practical sciences.

Consequently, he explained that there are three sorts of appre-   **63**
hensions in the practical sciences: first, apprehensions by the
senses; second, apprehensions by primary knowledge, beyond
what is apprehended by the senses; and third, what is apprehended
by investigation, consideration, and deliberation. It appears that
these very same modes of apprehension are present also in the

theoretical sciences. Hence all apprehensions become three: (1)
sense-perceptions, (2) primary cognitions by a knowledge beyond   5
what is supplied by the senses, and (3) cognitions resulting from
investigation and consideration. As to the cognitions resulting from
investigation and deliberation, their knowledge is originally acquired through primary cognitions—things that do not result from
investigation or deliberation. When they were being investigated
prior to being known, they were explored and called *sense-perceptions*. The primary cognitions employed to explain what one wants
to know are the *premises*. What one wants to know are the *questions*[1] (once they are known, he calls them *conclusions*). Hence all   10
these are originally three things.[2]

He explained that man cannot find the useful things, nor how
to labor nor with what to labor, without knowing the end
for the sake of which he should labor and without having that
end defined and present before him.[3] We know that man labors for
the sake of the soundness of those four things that were mentioned.
But if man proceeds to consider and investigate carefully which
one of these four is the end of the others, and which are the ones   15
pursued for the sake of this end—such as considering whether
the soundness of the body is for the sake of soundness of the
senses, or whether man pursues the soundness of his senses only
to use his senses for the soundness of his body (whence the senses
would be there solely for discerning that by which one attains the
soundness of the body), or whether all four are given only for
the sake of achieving every useful thing—there will be room here
for perplexity. For if the senses themselves are the end, one ought   20
not to permit the senses to serve what contributes to the soundness
of the body; and the body may even be an instrument for, or
subservient to, or a material constituent of, the senses. Hence the
power to discern well what leads to the soundness of the body,
the soundness of the power to labor, and the power to labor—   **64**
all will be for the sake of the soundness of the senses. Hence the
activity of the senses, and what man obtains by them, will themselves be the end.

One may, however, contradict all this. For we find ourselves
using the senses to apprehend what is useful for the soundness of
our bodies (and for the soundness [...] of the rest), or else we   5

place each one at the service of the other. Each one, then, is for
the sake of the other in a circular way. Hence either both should be
made the ends of each other—and how is this possible!—or a
part of each should be made the end! Man must understand the
truth of these things so that his labor will be directed toward
some definite end and not be for no end or for a thing that might
not itself be the end. Besides, why should man conclude that   10
the well-being of the body and the well-being of the senses (which
he finds innate in himself) are themselves the end? This also
requires evidence. For man is one of the beings not given their
perfection at the outset. He is rather one of those given only the
least of their perfections and, in addition, principles for laboring
(either by nature or by will and choice) toward perfection. Thus
the well-being of the body and the well-being of the senses given   15
to him might be similar to what is given him in childhood and
youth. To confine himself to the well-being of the body and the
soundness of the senses might be similar to confining himself to
childhood and youth. The soundness of the body might be pre-
paratory to another end. And the well-being of the senses might
be a principle to be used in the labor toward the end for which
the well-being of the body is but a preparation. Moreover, suppose
that man confined himself to the soundness of the body, to the
soundness of the senses, to the soundness of the capacity for   20
discerning what leads to the soundness of these two, and to the
soundness of the power to labor. Should he then proceed to consider what is the body's most excellent state of soundness, what
is the senses' most excellent state of soundness (because of which
it is asserted that the senses are as excellent as they can be),   **65**
what is the most excellent discernment, what is the most excellent
labor, and what is the most excellent capacity for performing it?
Here too there will be room for perplexity and diverse opinions.

   Then suppose he turns back once again to consider, and investigates carefully whether he ought to confine himself to the merely   5
necessary soundness of each one of the four things or whether
he ought to move on to the highest excellence of each. Is the soul's
desire to reach the highest excellence an intemperance of the
appetites and overreaching toward what is not for man to achieve
or do, or is acquiring the highest excellence of each one of these

the most perfectly human and the most appropriate thing for man?

Then if he sets out again to inquire, and considers how man's 10 soul calls upon him to understand the truth about what insinuates itself into one's own soul and how man desires to understand the causes of visible things: is this a desire for a human knowledge, or an intemperate appetite and overreaching toward improper knowledge and what is not human at all, or toward a thing that is truly human since it is more specifically human than those four? 15 Those four things man shares with other animals. For every animal has a body and senses and a power to discern somehow that by means of which it labors toward the soundness of its body and senses. But it does not have a desire to understand the causes of what it sees in the heaven and on earth, let alone having a sense of wonder about things whose causes it desires to understand.

Then if he considers, this also arises: why does man have a 20 natural desire to know these things, and why—if this knowledge is not human—was he made to have an innate desire for it and have primary cognitions that guide him to the truth about the things he desires to understand? Thus these things might be human. Or perhaps man might become more perfectly human, **66** either in his substance or in one of his attributes,[4] by knowing them. Their knowledge might itself be the substance of man or one of the acts of his substance. If it is one of the acts of his substance, and his substance to which this act belongs reaches its final perfection when it does this act, then he must know what the thing 5 is out of which this act emanates, and whether or not that itself is the end pursued in all the preceding labor.

Moreover, souls desire to know the things that are useful for what is necessary. (Knowledge is "excessive" and useless for what is necessary when things are known "excessively"; it is even more so when, qualitatively, the knowledge of useful and necessary things exceeds the measure necessary and useful to the necessary.) Is then the soul's desire for these things an overreaching by man, an intemperate appetite, and an infirmity attached to him by nature which must be removed and suppressed, or ought it to reach its completion? There is thus in all these questions room for perplexity and diversity of opinion, and topics for consideration. Man does not prefer one of these alternatives to the other without

some evidence to convince himself or others—and there is much 15
room for disagreement among the views of those who inquire into
them. Otherwise, to confine oneself to what might not be the end
condemns man to being confined to a rank of being beneath his
proper one.

Moreover, if man considers what is given him by nature—that
is, the soundness of body and senses, the capacity for discernment,
and the natural capacity to know, inquires into what is given him 20
also by will and the capacity for choice, and then investigates:
are the instruments given him by nature sufficient for achieving
the soundness of his body and senses as is the case with all animals,
plants, bodies, and natural bodies and parts? If these two [that is,
the body and the senses] are themselves the end, and the instru- 67
ments he possesses by nature are sufficient for achieving their
soundness, why then were will and choice given him? Will and
choice might thus exist because of infirmity and intemperance on
the part of nature; this intemperance ought then to be eliminated
and suppressed. But by what thing are this will and choice to be
suppressed, by will and choice or by nature? And if will and 5
choice are human, are they for the sake of the soundness of the
body and the senses that belong to him by nature? or is what
belongs to him by nature for the sake of what he acquires by
will and choice? or do nature and choice cooperate in order that
man achieve by them still another thing? And is the ultimate perfection attained by man the measure given him by nature? or is
nature, without will and choice, insufficient for man to achieve 10
his ultimate perfection? And is the perfection man reaches by will
and choice, or by both and nature, the perfection of what renders
him substantial, or is it the perfection of an attribute specific
to him?

In general, he ought to inquire what is the end that is the
ultimate perfection of man, whether it is his substance or an act
he performs after his substance is realized, and whether it is
realized for him by nature or whether nature supplies him only 15
with a material and a preparation for this perfection and a principle
and an instrument for his will to use in reaching it. Is then the
soundness of his body and senses the soundness of what renders
him substantial? Or is this absurd, since it is common to all

animals? Or are they both a preparation and an instrument for
what renders him substantial insofar as he is man? And does his
desire to know the things, to the knowledge of whose truth he
subsequently confines himself exclusively, perfect what renders   20
him substantial or perfect an attribute inherent to what renders
him substantial? Or is the knowledge of the truth one of the acts
of his own substance, because of which his substance is realized
in its final perfection?

Therefore man is forced to consider what is the substance of   **68**
man, what is his final perfection, and what is the act the performance of which leads to the final perfection of his substance. But
this implies knowing *what, by what,* and *how* is man, and *from
what* and *for what* he exists,⁵ so that when he labors, his labor   5
will be directed toward reaching this end. For if he does not, of
his own accord, learn what this perfection is, he will not know the
end for which he labors.

He explained that the proper human activity becomes known
only after one knows the purpose for which man is given a place
in the world as a part thereof and as that by which the totality of
the world is perfected—just as one cannot know the activity of
the weaver or the activity of the shoemaker or any other part   10
of the city without having known the purpose for which each one
of them is given a place in the city and the measure of its utility.
It is also impossible to know his purpose without knowing the purpose of the *whole* of which he is a *part,* and his place within the
whole and among all the parts of the whole—just as one does not
know the substance of the finger, its purpose, and its action, without knowing the hand, its substance, its purpose, and its place   15
among all the organs of the body, and without knowing beforehand the ultimate purpose of the entire body. For the purpose of
every part of a sum is either a part of the total purpose of the
whole, or else useful and necessary for realizing the ultimate
purpose of the whole.

Thus if man is a part of the world, and if we wish to understand his purpose and activity and use and place, first we have to   20
know the purpose of the whole world so that we may see clearly
what the purpose of man is, and also that man has to be a part of
the world because his purpose is necessary for realizing the ulti-   **69**

mate purpose of the whole world. Therefore if we wish to know the thing for which we ought to labor, we have to know the purpose of man and of the human perfection for which we ought to labor. This is why we are forced to know the purpose of the totality of the world; and we cannot know this without knowing   5 all the parts of the world and their principles—we have to know the *what, how, from what,* and *for what*[6] of the whole world as well as of every one of the parts that make up the world.

Since there are two things in man—one by nature and another by will—(*a*) when we wish to know the perfection he achieves by nature and the purpose of the perfection he achieves by   10 nature, we ought to know the natural whole of whose total purpose man's purpose is a natural part. If the world is natural (and many of its parts *are* natural), then for everything natural in the world (whether a whole or a part) and for whatever of this belongs to man by nature, a special inquiry ought to be set apart and pursued through a special investigation, theory, and science. This investi-   15 gation is called *natural* inquiry. (*b*) One should also inquire into what man and all other things have by virtue of will, and set apart a special investigation and science for the things that proceed from will. This is called *human* and *voluntary* science, since it is human and specific to man alone.[7]

Once we know the perfection for the sake of which man is made, and that this perfection is such that it is not achieved by   20 nature alone or by will alone but by nature and will jointly, then the acts and ways of life by which this perfection is attained will constitute the human and virtuous ways of life: they will be the virtues, beautiful things, acts, and ways of life that are noble. And   **70** the ones that deflect man from this perfection will constitute the acts and ways of life that are not human: they will be the vices and ugly things, and the base acts and ways of life. At this point we know that the former are what ought to be preferred and the latter what ought to be avoided.[8]

Because what is natural and innate to man precedes in time   5 both will and choice and what is in man by will and choice, the general inquiry into what exists by nature must precede the general inquiry into what exists by will and choice. Moreover, since it is not possible to understand will and choice and what is produced

by them without a prior understanding of what belongs to man   10
by nature, it follows also that the investigation of what exists by
nature should precede the investigation of what exists by will and
choice. And since the knowledge that man ought to possess and
according to the requirements of which he ought to act is the certain science and not any other, it follows that he should strive
after the certain science in everything he investigates, be it natural
or voluntary.

Therefore Aristotle saw fit to make known at the outset what   15
the certain science is, how many classes it has, in which subjects
it exists, how it exists, and by what and from what it exists in
every question; what beliefs are and what persuasion is, how many
are their classes, with regard to what they exist, and by what, how,
and from what they exist; what the things are that turn the investigator away from the certain science without his being aware
of it, how many they are, and what every one of them is; what   20
sort of argument is employed in instruction, of what it is composed, and how many classes it has; which one of the species
of the certain science is produced by each class of axiom used in
instruction; what class of the species of instruction produces certainty, and what class of the species of certainty it produces; what
class of instruction produces persuasion and imagination with   **71**
regard to the thing one intends to teach; what the art is by means
of which man acquires the power to teach certainty and to apprehend it, how many classes it has, and what each one of them is;
and what the art is from which the power over all the classes of
ways of instruction proceeds.

4   Then he explained afterwards how every class of men   5
ought to be instructed, what and by what they are instructed, and
which species of knowledge of these things ought to be given to
each class so that every man may know the end for which he
labors and hence be guided to the right course and not remain
dubious about what concerns him. Further, he made known what
the argument is with which one aims at sophistry, of what it is   10
composed, and how many classes it has. He made known the
species of bad qualities and styles produced in man's mind in accordance with the classes of sophisms, which of the species arises
out of which class of sophisms, and which of the species of the

true styles of science is produced through which species of sophisms. He made it known that these styles and qualities are five;[1] and he made known the ways in which one ought to guard against these sophistical approaches and with what to meet these classes 15 of sophisms.

He called the art that includes all these things the art of *logic*. For it improves the rational part of the soul, directs it toward certainty and the useful approaches to instruction and study, makes it discern the things that deflect from certainty and from what is useful in instruction and study, and also makes one discern how to articulate with the tongue and what manner 20 of argument is used in instruction and discern what manner of argument is used in sophistry with a view to using the former and avoiding the latter.

According to him, therefore, there emerge three sciences: the **72** science of logic, natural science, and voluntary science.[2] He let logic take the lead in the latter two sciences and gave it the authority to judge them and examine whatever takes place in them. Since the beings covered by these two sciences—that is, natural science 5 and voluntary science—are one in the genus,[3] and since the primary intention of the science of logic is to give an account of the above-mentioned things[4] with respect to the beings covered by natural science and voluntary science, he came to the view that the materials and subjects of the three sciences are subjects that are one in the genus.[5] And since the science of logic should precede the other two sciences, he began to enumerate at the outset the beings that are the materials and subjects of the three sciences 10 and that comprise what exists by nature and what exists by will. Those existing by nature are the subject of natural science;[6] those existing by will alone are the subject of voluntary science; and those that are common—that is, can be produced by either nature or will—are the subject of both sciences. The art of logic gives one a part of what he has to know about the subjects of these two 15 sciences. Hence the science of logic shares with these sciences their primary subjects and materials.

Therefore he began first to investigate and enumerate the instances of being from which the first premises are compounded, that contain the questions to be investigated, and that are the

primary significations of the expressions generally accepted by all. These are the [*summa genera*] whose being is attested by sense-perception and of which every intelligible is based on some   20
sensible thing. He confined all of them to ten genera, called them categories, and set them down in a book called in Greek *Katēgorías* and in Arabic *al-Maqūlāt* (*Categories*). These same genera are also the subjects of the natural sciences and, in general,   **73**
of the voluntary sciences[6] too.

5   Then afterwards he proceeded to make known what action the art of logic takes with regard to them and how it employs them. He began by making known how these classes are compounded so as to produce propositions that are premises, and   5
in how many classes they are compounded; then, how these very things are compounded so as to produce questions, and what is common to premises and questions and what separates them. Every question is in general the subject of two contradictory propositions, one of which is necessarily true and the other false; one does not know definitely which of the two is the true one, but supposes that one of the two is true and seeks to know which it is. Of   10
all propositions (*a*) some cannot not exist and some cannot exist— between them these make up the *necessary* propositions. (*b*) Others can exist or not exist; these are the *possible* propositions. (*c*) Still others either exist now or do not exist, could in the past have been as they are now or not have been, and may in the future be in this manner or not be; these are the *existential*.   15
That is to be found in a book by him which in Arabic is called *al-ʿIbārah* (*On Interpretation*) and in Greek *Perì ʿErmēneías.*

6   Then, after that, he made known how premises are compounded and paired together so that their combination produces a statement from which only one of the two contradictory propositions about every proposed question will necessarily and definitely follow; and in how many classes the original terms[1] (on   20
the basis of which the inquiry takes place and from which the investigation proceeds in the necessary, existential, and possible premises) are paired and compounded. He called the pair *com-*   **74**
pounded from the premises because the syllogism makes the truth of the whole question follow from them necessarily and always. He made known the manner in which, in every question put

before us, we can come upon the syllogism from which the truth
of that question will follow. He explained how, when a statement
is put before us, we examine it to know whether it is the kind of
statement from which the truth of the question, for the sake of   5
which the statement was made, follows. He made known the mode
of using these rules[2] in every rational art that uses reasoning and
investigation (whichever art this may be, whether it uses little or
much reasoning and investigation); and that every rational art
(for everything used in any of the rational arts, whichever it may
be, is employed by reasoning) uses some of these rules. Further,   10
he enumerated everything used in any investigation and reasoning
in every rational art. He thus explained that all the rules used
in reasoning and investigation are included in what he had
enumerated in this book of his. And he made it known, further,
that every argument in every art that employs instruction and
argument (whichever class of argument it may be, whether the   15
argument is intended for instruction, or sophistry and hindering
instruction) proceeds by using only these rules or some of them.
He placed these rules in a book he called in Greek ›*Analytiká;* in
Arabic it is *al-Taḥlīl bi-l-ʿaks (Analysis by Conversion).*

7   Then, after that, he made known what science is in
general: what the certain science is and how it is; how many
classes of the certain science there are; and that these are certainty *that* the thing is, certainty *why* the thing is, and certainty   20
about the substance of each one of the beings whose existence is
certain; how many classes there are of certainty *that* and *why*
the thing is, and that they are four: knowledge of (1) *what* it is,
(2–3) *from what* it is, and (4) *for the sake of what* it is.[1]

He made known how the questions with which each species   75
of the certain science is sought ought to be formulated, and which
materials and beings contain the questions and premises that fulfill these given states and conditions: they are the materials from
which the *necessary* propositions are compounded—that is, the
ones that cannot not exist and the ones that cannot exist; cer-   5
tainty cannot inhere in, or follow from, possible and existential
premises. He designated the premises that posit the thing's
existence the *principles of instruction* (for on their basis one knows
that the thing is, or knows *that* it is and *why* it is), while the

grounds of the thing's existence are called its *principles of being*.[2]

He made it known which species of the certain science exist   10
in which class of those materials [from which the necessary propositions and premises are compounded]—for not every species of
certainty can exist in any chance class of necessary beings: certainty as to *why* it is cannot be acquired about whatever has no
principle or cause of existence; in this case what is acquired is
only the certainty *that* it exists. Nor can every species of certainty
also exist with regard to every class of beings, for in many of them   15
there cannot be every species of certainty *why* it is, but only some
of them.[3] He made all these things known.

He made known what the art is that contains the materials
and beings with regard to which certainty exists (that is, the
materials from which the necessary propositions are compounded),   20
and distinguished it from the arts that comprise only the beings
with regard to which certainty is not possible. The latter arts
inquire into, or use, only the materials from which the possible
and existential propositions are compounded. He bestowed the
name *wisdom* specifically upon this art to the exclusion of others.   **76**
He maintained that the others that are called "wisdom" are wisdom only relatively and by comparison to this art: every other
art that follows the example of this art and emulates it in the
exhaustiveness of its knowledge and actions is called "wisdom" by
comparison to it, just as a man is given the name of an angel[4]
or of a virtuous man in the hope that he will emulate in his actions   5
the actions of the virtuous man or the angel[4] in question. Just as a
man may be given such a name because his activities and his
treatment of his subordinates correspond[5] to those of the virtuous
man or the angel in question, similarly the rest of the arts that
are called "wisdom" are only so called by analogy, comparison,
and likeness to this art, and because they are believed to possess
certain powers that are in fact possessed by this art.[6]   10

8   Then he explained how many divisions of this art there
are, how many species they have, what every one of their species
is, what class of materials and beings is contained in each, what
the questions are that pertain to it specifically, what the premises
are that are in it, how the questions and the first premises in it
ought to be, and what sort of investigation ought to be made in   *15*

each question or each species of this art. For every theoretical art is composed of some subjects that pertain to it specifically, of some questions that pertain to it specifically, and of first premises that pertain to it specifically. He made these things known with reference to all the species of the theoretical art that he called *wisdom*.

9   Then he made known the relative ranks of the species of the theoretical arts, what is common to them and what differ-   20 entiates them, which of them is emphatically prior and which of them is emphatically posterior, and which of them is subordinate to which. He investigated whether there is among them an art that precedes all the rest so that there will be no species emphatically prior to it and so that the rest will be subordinate to that one species. He explained in how many respects an art can be sub-   **77** ordinate to another art. And he explained that the one that was shown to be emphatically prior to the rest ought to be the most deserving of the name *wisdom* and the most deserving of the name *science*. Consequently, it is called *true wisdom, true science, the wisdom of wisdoms,* the *science of sciences,* and similar names.[1]

10   Then he made known how the first premises are used in   5 the discovery of each question in each art.

11   Then he made known the character of theoretical argument, how many classes it has, how every class ought to be used in each one of these species of the theoretical art, and which class of argument pertains specifically to which species of theoretical art;   10 what instruction is, its character, how many classes it has, of what it is composed, and which of its classes pertains specifically to which one of the species of the theoretical art.

12   Then afterwards he made known how the man ought to be in whom this faculty and this art can be realized, which psychical state he ought to possess by nature in order to be able to acquire this art and develop the faculty for performing its   15 functions, and how many these natural psychical states are; he who does not possess this natural state ought not to practice this art; if he does practice it, he will not develop the faculty for fulfilling its functions; if this is so, then he ought to be made to discern the human, natural, and voluntary things (which he had intended to explain to himself by means of this art) by other ways of instruction, and this ought to be established in his soul   20

by some other sort of knowledge; and men as a whole are equipped
by nature for different approaches to truth and for discerning   **78**
it and having it established in their souls by different sorts of
knowledge. Consequently, the one in whom the states that he
[Aristotle] enumerates in this book are natural and innate, belongs
to the elect by nature, and the one who does not possess these
states belongs by nature to the vulgar. The latter should know
the things with regard to which the certain science is possible by   5
some other approaches to knowledge.[1]

All this he set down in a book that he called *Second 'Analytiká*.

13 Then, after that, he gave an account of another art by
which man trains himself to acquire the capacity for quickly finding all possible syllogisms about any question at all in any theoretical art whatsoever, in order that such syllogisms as are found
by the investigator be ready for the application of the scientific   10
rules that he gave in the preceding book: that is, for being
examined by the investigator who will then accept what corresponds to those rules and reject what does not. For he saw that it
is extremely hard for man to hit upon the demonstration that leads
him to certainty regarding the question before him, or for his mind
to move immediately to inquire about the demonstration and consider it. Therefore he required a training art and a faculty to be   15
used as an instrument and servant or a preparation for the art of
certainty. He gave here an account of all the rules that can be
employed by the man who investigates when he is investigating and
reflecting, some for when he is investigating by himself and some
for when he is investigating with others. He formulated this art
primarily so that with it man will be equipped to show his power
of finding a syllogism quickly when he is investigating with others;
for, when he is equipped with this art, it also substantially develops 20
the faculty in him for using it when he is alone by himself, and
makes him exceedingly cautious and more quick-witted. For
when man imagines in everything he is investigating by himself that
there is as it were somebody else who is supervising or examin-   **79**
ing him, his mind will be made more quick-witted and he will be
more likely to be cautious. Therefore he equipped man with it so
as to employ it with others in question and answer. He called this
training and investigating art, which is an equipment for training

oneself and for becoming ready to approach science, the art of
dialectic. He set it down in a book of his known as *Topiká,* which
is the *Topics.*

  With the training art one conducts the preliminary investiga-   5
tion; it is a tool to be employed in question and answer. Therefore
when investigating by himself a man has no assurance that things
may not happen that cause him to err about the truth of the
question before him or that deflect him from the way of truth to
another. Although the training investigation does not move immediately to find the truth, by it man is nevertheless on the way to   10
truth; and it is more to be feared that he might err at this stage than
when he goes beyond the training art to the use of demonstration.
For man does not err, or hardly ever errs, when using demonstrations. On the other hand, so long as he is still engaged in the
training art, there is no assurance against error, since he is merely
investigating with rules and methods not corroborated yet by the
methods of certainty. Further, this art is a mere tool to be used   15
by man when questioning and answering others in certain kinds of
arguments whose purpose is neither instruction nor study, but only
a training by which each of the disputants makes a show of his
power in fending off what might be put forward to weaken or
mislead him, and in such an activity one is very likely to fall into
error.

  Therefore Aristotle needed to give, along with this training   20
art, an account of another art [that is, sophistry], permitting man
to understand everything that deflects him from the way of truth
when investigating by himself; and he had to make known all the   **80**
classes of argument that stand in the way of truth and cause him to
fancy that he is on the way of truth without being on the way to it.
He also formulated this art so that its arguments can be set before
the investigator instead of being put forward by him. Thus, while
he formulated the training art so that its arguments can be put
forward by both the investigator and his interlocutor, he formu-   5
lated it—this art by which the investigator guards against error
and whatever stands in the way of truth and turns him away from
it—so that its arguments could be presented by the interlocutor to
the investigator. As for the investigator himself, he did not enable
him to present the arguments of this art to his interlocutor;

instead he gave him still another power and art [that is, the art of examination],[1] by which to meet, and free himself from, the sophistical arguments set before him. Hence he gave the investi-   10
gator as it were two arts. One of them is the art whose arguments are presented to him by the interlocutor to divert him from pursuing the way to truth through the training art. The second is the art by which he meets and repels the arguments presented to him by the interlocutor—not for the sake of making his inter-locutor discern the truth or to engage with him in an investigation using the training art, but for the sake of repelling what obstructs him from employing the training art (whether by himself or with   15
others), and training himself without hindrance. He called the art that leads to error—with which he supplied the investigator so that the interlocutor might exercise it against him to prevent him from using the arguments of the training art—*sophistry*. As for the art he gave him to meet each of the things put before him by the interlocutor [that is, the art of examination], he formulated it as an art intermediate between the training art and the art of sophistry. For it is an art that, in its first intention, is not useful   20
when a man is investigating, either alone or with others. Nor is it a faculty whose function is to confute the sophist or to per-suade him. It is rather a faculty for repelling him and stopping him short of what he intends to set before the investigator or   **81**
before the audience, which may expect some benefit from the success of one of the disputants in an argument, or before the judges, be they one or a group. Therefore the man who answers the sophist ought to answer him sometimes only with what stops him in the eyes of the onlookers and the multitude and does it in a way comprehensible to the multitude and to the judges who   5
are present. In executing this action, he should aim either at truly stopping and silencing the sophist, or at stopping him in the eyes of the onlookers and judges who are present. Consequently, this is an art that is outside the sphere of the training art and the other argumentative arts.

The art of sophistry has six[2] aims with regard to whomever it argues against: (1) refutation, (2) perplexity,[3] (3) contentious-ness and the administration of flattery,[4] (4) reduction to solecism in speech and argument, (5) reduction to babbling in the argu-   10

ment, and (6) silencing, that is, to prevent someone from speaking altogether—even though the man who is being argued against were able to speak—by reducing him to a condition in or because of which he will prefer silence. (1) To refute is to reduce somebody to a thesis contrary to the one he had laid down, by means of things that falsify his original thesis. These things are the same as the ones that, when a man uses them by himself, lead him astray   15
and deflect him from the truth toward what contradicts it by causing him to reject the truth and prefer what contradicts it. (2) Perplexity is something else. For perplexity means that a man is caught in bewilderment between two contradictory convictions because the sophist presents him with something from which one of the two convictions follows, and presents him also with something else from which the contradictory conviction follows. That is, when he is asked concerning a thing: "Is it so, or is it not so?"   20
whichever he answers, a refutation follows. This is the method of perplexity. Hence to refute someone is to transfer him positively from one of the two contradictories to the other, while to perplex   **82**
him is to transfer his mind from the first to the second, from the second to the first, and from the first to the second: soon the assertions following from the two contradictories possess equal force, at which time perplexity occurs. (3) As to confounding and contentiousness, it is to reduce a man to rejecting things that are perfectly obvious by raising doubts about those aspects of them   5
that are self-evident, so that the man forfeits every principle of instruction and study, and even goes beyond this to suspect sense-perception regarding things whose validity is attested to by sense-perception, to suspect what is generally accepted, and to suspect things valid by induction. For this is one of the functions of the art of sophistry. Its intention is to obstruct investigation and obstruct a thing's apprehension by an investigation. These three   10
styles affect the soul; they are very bad styles; and they are produced by this sophistical art alone. As to the remaining three styles, they are twists only of language and not of the mind, while the former three are twists of the mind. (4) For when a man is reduced to solecism in argument, he is either reduced to solecism   15
absolutely by nature or custom, or reduced to solecism in the language of the nation whose language is used in the argument

against him. Likewise, solecism follows: (*a*) absolutely, in which case it has to do with things that are hard to express adequately and things that, when combined, lead one to fancy that the content of the proposition expressing the combination is absurd. This occurs in all languages. Or (*b*) it may occur in the language belonging to a certain nation. Hence a man is reduced to solecism   20 absolutely when he is reduced to absurdity regarding the content of a generally accepted and perfectly common expression. But when that absurdity follows from a combination in the language of   **83** a certain nation specifically, and the two partners to the argument are talking in the language of that nation, the solecism that follows is relative to the language of that nation. (5) Reduction to babbling is similar. For solecism means to express things inadequately, and the absurdity of the meaning follows because of the inadequacy of the expression. Babbling means that the expression exceeds the meaning, and the absurdity follows from the super-   5 imposition of one meaning on another. For there are numerous ideas that cannot be expressed except by means of an expression that is inevitably repetitive, either actually or potentially, and this leads one to fancy a repetition in the meaning, from which repetition in the meaning an absurdity follows. It is only in or through such expressions that the sophist can reduce someone to babbling. (6) As to silencing, it is the meanest function of sophistry, for it   10 proceeds by causing fear or shame or other passions. Aristotle enumerated with regard to every one of those styles all the components of the argument by means of which the sophist reaches his purpose.

14   Then he gave an account of the rules that enable man, provided he keeps to them and trains himself in them, to contend   15 with the sophist in each one of these styles by means of obstructing him from executing his action.

All this is to be found in a book of his that he called *Sophistiká*. Its purpose is to make the training art secure and prevent the preparation for truth from being dissipated. For this art of sophistry indeed contradicts the art of dialectic—that is, the training art—and obstructs it from performing its functions, which are the way to truth and to certainty. It is in this way that the   20 art presented by Aristotle in this book of his is useful with refer-   **84** ence to truth. It defends the instrument and servant of truth, for dialectic is the instrument and servant of the certain science.

These, then, are the methods by means of which Aristotle canvassed the certain science, gave an account of the way to it, and intercepted what stands in its way.

ii   5

15   When he had achieved this much of the certain science, he afterwards gave an account of the powers and the arts by which man comes to possess the faculty for instructing whoever is not to use the science of logic or to be given the certain science. These are two groups: a group that by nature does not possess the psychical states [mentioned in the *Posterior Analytics*];[1] and a   10 group that does possess these states by nature, but in which they have been corrupted and obstructed in performing their functions by being accustomed to, and busied with, other functions. For Aristotle is of the opinion that he who knows with certainty the end and that by which one arrives at the end—that is, he who is equipped for truth by nature—ought to labor for a human end. But he is also of the opinion that whenever the others labor, their labor, too, ought to be directed toward what they know to the   15 measure of their ability to know. Therefore he did not confine himself in instruction to giving an account of how to instruct the one who should be given certainty about the beings, but gave also an account of the art and the power by which to instruct all others in these very same beings.

Therefore he gave an account of the art [that is, rhetoric] that enables man to persuade the multitude regarding (*a*) all   20 theoretical things and (*b*) those practical things in which it is customary to confine oneself to using persuasive arguments based   **85** on particular examples drawn from men's activities when conducting their public business—that is, the activities through which they labor together toward the end for the sake of which man is made.[2]

16   Then afterwards he gave an account of the art [that is, poetics] that enables man to project images of the things that   5

became evident in the certain demonstrations in the theoretical
arts, to imitate them by means of their similitudes, and to project
images of, and imitate, all the other particular things in which it
is customary to employ images and imitation through speech.
For image-making and imitation by means of similitudes is one
way to instruct the multitude and the vulgar in a large number of
difficult theoretical things so as to produce in their souls the
impressions of these things by way of their similitudes. The vulgar   10
need not conceive and comprehend these things as they are. It is
enough if they comprehend and intellect them by means of what
corresponds to them. For to comprehend them in their essences
as they are is extremely hard except for whoever devotes himself
to the theoretical sciences alone.[1]

He did not, then, omit anything by which it is possible to
arrive at the knowledge of the end after which he strove, or the
perfection that he made the primary goal of his knowledge and
toil, or anything that makes it easier for him to instruct others, to   15
whatever class of men they may belong; no, he treated all of them
fully. He trained himself fully in all of them, he made use of the
tools he gave to man to employ by himself, and he made use of
the tools he gave to man to employ with others, either in teaching
and guidance or in disputing and repelling whoever contends
against the instruments of truth. He called the faculty resulting
from these arts the *logical* faculty.[2]

iii   20

17 When he had completed these matters, he set out upon
natural science. He turned once again to the instances of being   **86**
that he enumerated in the *Categories*. He took them and assumed
that they *are* in the manner attested to by sense-perception: in
the manner, that is, in which we assume that these categories
are when we use some of them to inform ourselves about the
others, to inquire about the others, and to acquaint ourselves
with the others—which man does either by himself or in argument   5
with another. But this does not mean that they *are* by nature for
us to use in this manner. No, he assumed at the outset that the

natural beings [that is, subjects] are natures, and essences constituted by nature; the categories are their marks that we know
and perceive by the senses. These are *logical* states with which
we have designated the natural beings. But the natural beings are
not beings only so far as they possess such states—which is how   10
they were taken in logic. For in logic, it was not assumed that
they are natures abstracted from these states and that these are
their first marks, but that they *are* in this manner and that these
states are one of the two parts of their being so far as they
are logical.

Now sense-perception attests to the multiplicity of natural
things. This multiplicity is perceived through sense-perception in   15
two ways. First, sense-perception apprehends a multiplicity of
natural things because the [same things] are dispersed in separate
places; it distinguishes them from each other by virtue of the different places they occupy. This, then, is the first kind of multiplicity; it is better known. Second, the multiplicity of natural things
is apprehended through sense-perception of a single object. This
happens: (*a*) when one particular sense-organ apprehends (1)
a multiplicity of things that are not contrary (such as to touch a
single body and apprehend that it is hot and hard and rough),
or (2) a multiplicity of things that are contraries (such as that a   20
single body is hot and cold, hard and soft, rough and smooth, and
so on with regard to the other objects of sense-perception); (*b*)
when several sense-organs are employed in apprehending the
multiplicity of things (such as that a given object is both hot and
white—for one of these is apprehended by touch and the other   **87**
by sight, and so on with regard to the other senses).

18   Then he explained how much knowledge is acquired by
sense-perception about each of the sensible things independently
and by what marks the one can be distinguished from the other.
Furthermore, sense-perception attests and apprehends that all or   5
most of them change and pass from one place to another and from
one state to another: something that is white becomes black, many
contraries follow consecutively upon it, and yet there exists dur-
ing this consecutive process one persisting and unvarying thing that
carries these consecutive states and is their subject. For the time being he called the subject upon which the varying states follow con-

secutively and that is persistent through this process *substance,* and
he called the variable, consecutive states *attributes.* These, then, are   10
the natural things apprehended and attested to by sense-perception.

As to what the categories of natural beings disclose, when
some categories supply information about the others, and when
some of them are used to inquire, or seek information, about the
others, it is as follows: one of their categories informs us only
what the thing is and does not provide us with any other type of
information, while the others inform us *how much* it is, *how* it is, or   15
something else that is extraneous to *what* the sensible thing is.

Moreover, we also discover in ourselves through the intelligibles of these natural things that these beings are many because of
the multiplicity of their places; however, we can only obtain this
conception of them by drawing an analogy between the intelligibles
and the corresponding sensible things. But as for us, when we consider the character that these intelligibles assume in ourselves, we   20
find that we conceive of the multiplicity of the natural beings solely
in terms of the multiplicity of what we intellect about them. Thus
what we sense as one thing is conceived by us—insofar as it is intelligible—as many, so that the multiplicity that we conceive in virtue of what we intellect of it becomes similar to the multiplicity of   **88**
sensible things due to the multiplicity of their places. Hence the
same thing is asserted to be one subject, and many attributes and
predicates; and out of that thing (the one subject) every one of
those attributes is construed as existent, so that we say: "This
given thing—which is Zayd—*is* an animal, *is* white, and *is* tall";   5
thus we perceive intellectually that it exists in many ways.

However, once we distinguish what each one of these many
intelligible predicates tells of the same thing, we posit the one
through the intellection of which we hold that we have intellected
what the thing is as the "substance" of the thing. Then if this very
thing, which we asserted to be the "substance," makes known (with   10
respect to the substratum of *what* it is) *how much* it is, *how* it is,
or some other state besides what it is, we assert that this thing—
this intelligible essence—is a "substance" insofar as it makes
known *what* is and an "attribute" insofar as it gives another description besides *what* is. And if a given thing is sensible, and many   15

intelligibles are attributed to it, among which there is an intelligible that makes known to us *what* that sensible thing is without making known to us anything at all regarding anything else (either *how much* it is, *how* it is, or any of the other states that are not *what* it is), we assert it to be "substance" without qualification—not a relative substance, as it were, a substance of one thing and an attribute in another thing. Hence, whenever an intelligible nature is of this description, we call it "substance" without qualification. Every- 20 thing else is evidently an attribute in relation to what is substance without qualification; the other, which we call "substance" in relation to it, we call "substance" to the extent that it is similar to this substance: that is, insofar as it makes known *what* a thing is. **89** Let substance, then, be what is substance without qualification; those others, he called in general *attributes in the substance*. (This division subsequently receives as its complement the preceding division in logic: that is, of the attributes in the substance, some are *essentially* in the substance and some are in it *accidentally*. 5 Of the essential, some are *primary* and others are *secondary*.) *This* substance is not disjoined from an attribute, either in sense-perception or when intellected. The intellect may divorce it from its attributes, and the attributes from each other, not because this is how they *are,* but only so that it may perceive the substance independently. This, then, is the being attested to by sense-perception and attested to by the way we as human beings use these 10 things.

Aristotle simply assumed these things on the basis of the primary knowledge we have of them. Accordingly, those of them that do not at all exist by the will of man, he assumed to be *natural* beings. He explained that each one of the species of this substance whose existence is not at all due to human will has a "whatness" [that is, a shape or form corresponding to its definition][1] in virtue of which its specific substance is rendered substantial and in virtue of which its essence differentiates itself from 15 every other species. He called the whatness of each one of them, insofar as it is a substance, *its nature*. He explained that every one of these species is constituted by its nature. (It is apparent that the whatness of every species is that for which the species performs the activity generated from it; it is also the cause of all the

essential attributes in it—be that attribute a movement, a quantity, a quality, a position, or something else—just as the whatness of   20
the wall is that for which it supports the roof and admits the attributes that walls as walls admit.) He called the species of substances, the constitution of every one of which is by "nature" in this special sense, *natural* substances; and he called the essential   **90**
attributes in every one of them *natural* attributes. It was not his intention to investigate them only to the extent to which he apprehended them by sense-perception or to the extent to which he had innate apprehension of their intelligibles; rather, he sets them forth as first premises in order to investigate their properties that he mentioned in the logic, following the method that he stated there.   5

iv

19   When he decided to proceed with this investigation, he found statements that contradict the appearance of these things in sense-perception and contradict the actual use of what is intellected about them. These statements raise doubts whether beings change and are different from each other. They affirm that difference   10
and change are not possible among beings in virtue of *being* and insofar as they *are*, but only in virtue of not being. For what is not the thing, has become what this thing is not, only in virtue of the latter's nonbeing. There are, then, in these particular sensible things, particular nonbeings in virtue of which the particular beings differ from each other. Therefore, if it is assumed that they *are* without qualification, the difference between one being and   15
another is in virtue of nonbeing; but this does not exist at all, and what does not exist is not a thing. Therefore what is believed to be difference does not exist, for it would be in virtue of nonbeing and in virtue of what is not, and what is not is not being. Therefore difference and change do not exist. Since multiplicity is in virtue of difference, multiplicity therefore does not exist in the being. Therefore, *being* is one. Hence it is precluded that the   20
same thing be endowed with many properties, and that each of these signify something other than what the others signify about   **91**
that same thing; what the many expressions signify becomes nu-

merically one; indeed there exists neither word nor speech. It is this hypothesis that gave rise to the statements that contradict both what is attested to by sense-perception and what we find when we make use of the intelligibles of these sensible things.

First he refuted those statements. He explained that they are 5 fallacies and that they do not abolish any of those premises. The latter do not become valid by his refuting the contradictory statements. They are valid by sense-perception and by virtue of what is intellected of them.

20 Then, after that, he proceeded to inquire into them. He found that each of the things he called *substance* extends in all directions, having length, width, and depth. He called them, 10 insofar as they are endowed with the property of extending in all the directions, at times *bodies* and at times *bodily substances.* Hence natural beings become bodies and attributes, and bodily substances (or substances that admit of assuming a bodily form) and attributes in them.

These, then, are the subjects of natural science. He takes the evident premises regarding these things and first uses the dialectical methods to investigate them up to that point in the investiga- 15 tion of each of them at which the dialectical faculty can proceed no further. Thereupon he goes over them once again with the scientific rules and sifts them. Those that fulfill the requirements of the premises leading to certainty, he puts forward as demonstrations. And those that do not fulfill these requirements, he leaves as they are, set down in his books as provisions for the investigators who will come after him, so that in their quest for the certain science they may investigate what is given there about the material to be 20 investigated, the method of investigation, and the use of dialectic. This, then, is the sum of his inquiry into natural science. For in everything into which he inquires, he brings together two approaches—dialectic and the certain science—until he finally 92 arrives at what is certain about everything he aims to know.

He begins first by using this method: he gives in this science an account of some universal hypotheses, which are the most general hypotheses regarding natural beings. These hypotheses are universal propositions, premises, and rules covering all natural beings. (In all subsequent things, he uses the principles of instruc- 5 tion.) They are not self-evident first premises, but extremely universal propositions that are not known at the outset: they are to become evident by means of demonstrations composed of self-evident first premises. He employs the dialectical faculty in investigating them; when their knowledge is attained, they are taken and put forward as a provision to be used in the explanation of all the natural things that are investigated afterwards.

The first of these hypotheses are the universal rules regarding   10
the principles of being of all bodily substances: *what* they are, and *why* they are. He first explained that each one of them has two principles: a principle in virtue of which it is potentially, which is called the *material,* and a principle in virtue of which it is in act, which he called the *form.*

21   Then he explained that the principle that exists potentially [that is, the material] is not sufficient for making what is   15
potential come to be in act, but that there must necessarily be a third principle to move it from potentiality to actuality. He called this principle the *agent* principle.

22   Then he explained that everything that moves and changes must necessarily be moving toward an end and a definite purpose; everything that is a bodily substance is either for a pur-   20
pose and an end, or is a concomitant of, and adheres to, a thing that is for a certain purpose and end. Therefore it became evident to him that bodily substances have all the principles; all the prin-ciples of their being are of four kinds, no more and no less; and   **93**
these four are the material, the whatness [that is, the form],[1] the agent, and the end.

23   Then he made known what nature is, and what it is according to all those who discourse about nature. First, he made known its whatness in the most general statement that comprises all that nature is said to be according to the ancient physicists;   5
what nature is said to be according to himself as the sum of these principles; how one can sum up what nature means; what is the rank of the principle called *nature;* what is the meaning of our saying *natural things;* in what way it is said that the principles of the being of these things are *natural* principles; what is the mean-ing of our saying *according to nature;* what is the meaning of what is *by nature* and of what is *not according to nature;* [what is the   10

meaning of] *comprehensive natural theory;* by means of what the *natural* theory of these beings is distinguished from the theory that is not natural; the rules regarding the ranking of the four principles in relation to each other (which of them are emphatically prior and which emphatically posterior); and which of them are more dominant in the beings he is investigating and pertain more specifically to natural things. These, then, are the first hypotheses and the first rules.

24   Then afterwards he gave an account of certain rules and   15
hypotheses regarding the bodily substances themselves. He investigated first what *body* is insofar as it is extended in all directions, what extension is, by virtue of what the body is extended, and what the cause of this extension is: whether it is the interval between the parts of what is extended and the proximity of their positions or something else; and, in general, *what* extension is, *how* it is, and *from what* it is.

25   Then he investigated afterwards the substance of the   20
natural bodily thing. Does the fact that it is a *substance* mean that it is extended in all directions? Does the fact that it is a body and is extended mean that it is a substance (a subject) for all   **94**
the attributes? Or does the fact that it is a body and is extended mean that it is the *material* from which the species of substance are generated and in which the forms and the attributes succeed while it remains unchanging? Or does the fact that it is extended mean that it is a *material substance* whose extension is in virtue of its having length and width and depth? He explained that *sub-*   5
stance is something other than what is extended: *extended* does not signify its essence insofar as it is a substance. Our saying *extended* indicates an idea similar to our saying that it is *white*. Our saying the substance is *substance without qualification* does not mean that it is extended, nor does it mean that it has length and width and depth, but other properties of the substance. The idea of the *extended* and the idea of *extension* do not mean either the material or the form of the bodily substance (indeed its   10
material in itself is a nonbody, and similarly its form). Extension in all directions inheres in the *composite* of the two: this extension exists in the composite as something whose being adheres to the latter's form, since it is in virtue of the form that the substance

is, perfectly and in act. The material of the natural substance is
not disjoined from its form (therefore, substance is not composed   15
of any extension). Extension—and length and width and depth—
is the most prior *attribute* in it: this attribute is engendered in it,
changes, increases, and decreases, like all the other attributes in
the natural substance.

26   Then he investigated whether or not there is a natural
bodily substance boundlessly extended in magnitude. He explained
that no natural bodily substance is infinitely extended in magni-   20
tude, but that every natural bodily substance is of finite magnitude
and extension. He explained that there is an infinity of the finite in
natural things, but that it has a meaning and a mode other than
what infinity is believed to mean by those who have discoursed
about natural things. He summed up what that meaning is, and   **95**
how and in what it is.

27   Then he investigated what motion is, and its being and
whatness. Since motion has a whatness that signifies its definition,
and has species; since it is *from* a thing and *to* a thing, and at a
distance and in time; since it is an attribute in a bodily substance;
and since it exists from a mover—he had to investigate every one   5
of these and its essential consequences: to summarize *what* it is,
for what it is, and *how* it is, and to make its essential consequences
known. And since each of these things entails many consequences
for motion, since motion entails consequences for each of these,
and since motion entails consequences for the moving bodies, he
began to investigate what consequence each of these entails for   10
motion and what consequence motion entails for each of them.

Therefore he investigated what place is. He summed up the
concomitants of place that adhere to its whatness. He investigated
whether the body is in need of place in order to exist as body, or
rather needs place to realize one of its attributes.

He investigated whether or not for motion to exist the moving   15
thing requires void. He explained that void is not required by
the moving thing or for the existence of motion; and, in general,
that no void at all is required for the existence of a natural thing,
be it a substance or an attribute.

28   Then he explained generally that void cannot in any way   20
exist.

29   Then he made known what time is, and all that is concomitant to time itself, to motion, and to natural beings; and **96** whether natural beings or motion, to exist, have to exist in time, or whether time is a consequent attribute not required for the existence of any being at all.

He made known the hypotheses and rules regarding all the consequences that every one of these things entails for motion   5 and all the consequences that motion entails for these things.

30   Then he investigated, among other things, how the whatness of motion entails that successive, periodic motion be boundless.

31   Then he gave an account of many axioms regarding bodies that follow from their motion and from the principles that move them. It follows that the moving bodies present before us   10 are moved by other bodies that are together and in contact with them, and these in turn by others together and in contact with them, and the latter in turn by others together and in contact with them; the bodies that move each other are contiguous in their positions or in contact, succeeding each other; and this succession is infinite in number.

He had previously given an account of the modes and ways in which the natural body, by its nature, moves another body: 15 the last of the bodies, which moves the moving things that come after it, must also be moving, but only with local motion exclusively (its local motion not being straight but circular, occupying the distance that is the circumference of all the other natural moving bodies); there cannot be beyond this body another that moves it. He had previously explained also that there cannot at all be an   20 infinite body. It follows from this that there is here a finite body that moves all the natural bodies, and that the outermost of what **97** this body includes is moving in a circular motion around the rest.

32   Then he investigated whether this body, which moves in a circular motion, moves without a mover or has a mover. He explained that it has a mover.

33   Then he investigated whether or not the principles that   5 move the bodies moving in a circular motion by nature are themselves bodies or whether they are nonbodily essences that are, however, *in* a material and a body.

v

34   When he had investigated the case closely, it became
obvious to him that that which gives circular motion to the bodies   10
at the limits is a certain being that cannot be a nature or a
natural thing, or a body or in a body, or ever in a material at all;
and that he ought to inquire into it by means of another investigation and another theory, different from natural investigation
and theory.

This is the sum of the axioms of natural science that he
presented in a book of his called *Lectures on Physics*.   15

35   Then in another book he began from the final point
reached in *Lectures on Physics*. This is that it follows necessarily
that there is a body moving circularly at the circumference sur-
rounding all the other bodies, and in which there is no void at all;
what is inside that body is bodies that are continuous and in
contact, since there is no void at all in the interval between them.   **98**
He called the totality containing all the bodies that are continuous or in contact the *world*. He investigated first whether the
world is homogeneous or heterogeneous.

36   Then he investigated whether the sum of the bodies in
the world includes certain bodies that were the first to constitute   5
the world—so that they are the *primary parts* of the world, so
that if one of them were missing the world would vanish or
become defective and would not be a world. He explained that
there are certain bodies that were the first to constitute the world,
and that they alone are the primary parts of the world.

vi

37   When this had become evident to him, he proceeded   10
to discourse about these primary bodies and to speak of the others
posterior to them. First, he investigated how many such *primary
bodies* there are among the bodies that constitute the world at
the outset. Since there is among these bodies a body that moves in
a circular motion around the rest, it follows necessarily that there

are first two places: a central place, and another which is around   15
the center. It follows that the bodies that move by the most simple
local motion are three: what moves about the center, what moves
toward the center, and what moves away from the center; and
that these three are dissimilar in their species, and in contact,
since there is no void at all in the interval between them.

38   Then he investigated these three movements, and whether
what moves out of the center is of one or more than one   **99**
species. It became evident to him that it is made up of three
species. He investigated each one of them, the substance of each
class, and all the essential attributes in each. For each of them
he gave an account of *what* it is, *from what* it is, and *for what*.
He explained that they are the *simple* bodies. He explained that   5
there are five *primary simple bodies* that constitute the world.
He made known their ranks and their positions in the world,
and the ranks and positions of each relative to the others. He
made known the parts of all of them that have parts, and the
ranks of their parts: one of them is the outermost body that moves
in a circular motion: the remaining four have common material
but are different in their forms: the fifth differs from these four   10
in both its material and its form, and is the cause of the existence
of these four, of their constitution, of the continuity of their
being, of their positions, and of their ranks: these four are the
elements from which all the bodies below that outermost body
come into being, and these elements are also generated from each
other and not generated from a body simpler than they or from any
body at all.   15

All this is to be found in a book of his that he called *On the
Heaven and the World.*

39   Then he began, in another book, from the final point
reached in *On the Heaven and the World.* This is that these four
[simple bodies] are elements, they generate themselves, and they
are generated from each other because they are the primary natural substances; their materials are one in species, and taken in   20
their consecutive order, the material of each element is identical
with the material of the next. Since they become elements only
because each is generated from the other; since the rest of the generated bodies are but generated from them; and since there are   **100**

in them principles and powers in virtue of which they are generated from each other and because of which the rest of the generated bodies come into being; since it was stated [by some][1] that
generation and corruption are alteration, and that generation is
growing and corruption is diminishing; since, when it becomes
evident what generation is, it follows necessarily that, in a thing
whose parts are generated from each other, one part be acted on   5
and another part act on it; since it follows necessarily that, in a
thing one of whose parts is acted on by another, the parts be in
contact; and since the things generated from these elements are
but generated from the combination of these four elements, the
mixture of some of them with others, and their blending together
—he needed, therefore, to investigate first what generation and
corruption are, in what way they take place, and in what they take   10
place, and to show that generation and corruption are not association and dissociation. He stated what alteration is, and that it is
other than generation and corruption.

40   Then he followed this with the investigation of growth
and diminution. He made an exhaustive investigation of them and
showed that they are other than generation and corruption.

41   Then he followed this with the investigation of the contact of bodies that act on each other and are acted on by each   15
other. He investigated also the bodies that act on others and are
acted on by others.

42   Then he investigated what action is and what passion
[that is, to be acted on] is, and showed that they take place in
sensible qualities. He explained in what way this takes place.

43   Then he followed this with the investigation of the com-   20
bination, mixture, and blending by which all the bodies generated
from the elements come into being.

vii   **101**

44   When he had exhausted all of this, he investigated afterwards in what manner the four bodies[1] are elements and in what
sense they are "elements": whether there are in them principles
or powers by virtue of which they become elements, whether they

are elements by virtue of their substances or by virtue of natural   5
powers in them other than their substances, whether they are
primary elements or they possess other elements prior to them,
and whether the powers by virtue of which they have become elements make them boundless or finite. This investigation of whether
they are boundless differs from the previous investigations. For
it was previously investigated in the former book whether or not
each one of them is boundless in magnitude and whether or not   10
the *primary* bodies that constitute the world are of infinite number.[2] What he investigates here, on the other hand, is whether
or not they are infinite in their mode as elements and in respect
to the powers[3] that made them into elements. An example of this
is water, since it is one of these four bodies. For [if it is bound-
less], it could then have one power in virtue of which it is a
single element (thus water is a single element by *this* power),   15
and another power in virtue of which it is many elements. Similarly,
water could have a power in virtue of which it is an infinite
number of elements. This would be in one of two ways: either
it will dissociate into waters whose number is infinite, or there
will be in every water an infinite number of powers in virtue of
each of which that water is a separate element. He explained
regarding all this that it is impossible; they cannot be more than   20
four; and it is because of their powers that the elements are finite
in number. He investigated how many these powers are until he
found their number. He made it known that these are the powers
by which the elements act on each other and are acted on by each
other: the first step of a thing's generation is that it act on some
sensible qualities and then undergo a change in substance; but,   **102**
as it has become evident previously, the thing must also be acted
on with respect to the qualities by virtue of which the four bodies
have become elements.

45   Then he investigated whether every one of them is
generated from every one, or three of them are generated from one.   5

46   Then he investigated their generation from each other:
how, and by what mode, this takes place.

47   Then he investigated the generation of the rest of the
bodies from them: how they are generated, how they are com-

bined, and according to which type of combination they are
combined so that from their combination the rest of the gen-   10
erated bodies can come into being.

viii

48   When he had exhausted all of this, he investigated whether
the powers and the principles, in virtue of which the elements
act on each other and are acted on by each other, are sufficient
for their generation from each other and the generation of the
other bodies from them. Are the positions they occupy in rela-   15
tion to each other in the primary regions of the world sufficient
for their combination with, and addition to, each other of themselves, so that the other remaining bodies can come into being
from them? Or are they in all of this in need of another agent
from outside to impart to them other powers and bring them
close together so that they combine, and to provide them with
principles for generating a thing other than they? He explained
that they are not sufficient, in their substances or in any of their   **103**
states, without another agent besides them.

49   Then at this point he investigated the agent principles
that supply the elements with the powers in virtue of which they
act on each other and bring them close together so that they
become combined. He explained that their agent principles are   5
the heavenly bodies; and he made known how, and in how many
ways, they act as agents.

50   Then he investigated what distinguishes the materials
that generally constitute the generated and corrupted bodies, and
showed that they are the materials of the elements exclusively.

51   Then he investigated the nature in virtue of which all
that comes into being exists in act.

52   Then, after that, he investigated the end and the pur-   10
pose for which these species are subjected to generation and
corruption, the cause of their being generated from each other,
why those of them that recur are generated from what has gone
before, and why generated things succeed each other consecu-

tively. He examined the purpose and the end for which these species, to the exclusion of others, exist subject to generation and corruption.

53   Then he investigated whether corrupted things recur and   15 thus exist again as they were, or none of them recurs at all, or some recur and others do not recur; and in what way that which recurs recurs: does it recur many times or once? and does what is generated and corrupted recur a finite or an infinite number of times?

All these things are to be found in a book of his known as *On Generation and Corruption.*

54   Then afterwards[1] he investigated what will now be men-   20 tioned regarding these elements. This is that since these elements **104** are contraries (in respect of both the whatness in virtue of which they are in act and the powers in virtue of which they are elements), since they act on each other and are acted on by each other, and since they are together, it is possible that each element is [distributed according to the following scale]: (*a*) some of it is about to reach, or has already reached, the limits of perfection   5 with respect to what renders it substantial and with respect to its essence,[2] and also has reached the ultimate and most extreme degree with respect to the power by virtue of which it is a pure element; (*b*) some of it is below the former in perfection, (*c*) some of it is below the latter, and so on—until it terminates in having the least possible degree of its essence, so that, were it to be deprived of this, its essence would become the essence of another element in the lowest possible degree in which the other can have its essence. This last will occur when it is deprived of   10 its own essence, which can happen only in two ways. First, the material that admits what constitutes its essence will admit a little of the essence of the other, its contrary; at this stage, the action of the essence of its contrary does not manifest itself. Then it keeps admitting more of the essence of its contrary until the action it generates becomes the action of the essence of its contrary, at which point it is given the definition of its con- trary rather than its own definition as before. Or, second, this [diminution of its essence] takes place without its admitting any-   15 thing of the essence of its contrary. He investigated whether, when

they are still short of having their highest perfection, the elements are elements in virtue of their own powers.[3]

55   Then, after that, he investigated in what way the elements are together. Are (1) the parts of every one cut into small pieces dispersed in the intervals of the others? Or is (2) the sum of each body distinguished by a place different from the place of the other? so that (*a*) the one in the *center* is one of these four   20
bodies, pure, and not including among its parts any part of the other three, (*b*) the one in the *upper* place of the world is also in this condition, and (*c*) the one in the interval *between* the upper and the center is also in this manner: so that the body **105**
in contact with the heavenly bodies is one of the elements, the one below it and together with it is another, and similarly until they terminate in the lowest place, which is the center. Or does the latter alternative—were it possible—require that the parts of each element be also in the parts of every one of the others, and that the parts of the one element be in each other? He   5
explained that they are together in the two ways.

56   Then he explained in what condition the body in contact with the heavenly bodies ought to be. He explained that it ought to have the purest essence and come close to being endowed with the extreme of essence and power: the body that is *there* must be the lightest, the most intense in heat and dryness, and the   10
least mixed with others; then the next element together with [that is, next to] it must be less extreme in its essence and power, indeed it must not be of extreme but rather of defective essence and incomplete power; and then the nearer it is to the center, the less should be the power in virtue of which it is an element and the essence that renders it substantial.

57   Then he required that the element together with [that   15
is, next to] the latter be related to it in the same manner, until they terminate in the element in the center. He required that this last one, especially, ought to be the most defective and the most mixed with others, so that the three elements be mixed with it in many types of mixtures. He gave an account of the cause of all this with respect to the heavenly bodies, which are their   20
agents, and with respect to the material and whatever inheres in it.

58   Then he explained that these theoretical requirements

are in agreement with what is found out about the elements
by observation.

59 Then he investigated afterwards what one ought to **106**
call these elements if they are pure, having the essence belonging
to them alone (without their contrary being in any way mixed
with them), and are most extreme in the powers in virtue of
which they are elements. He did not find names by which to call
them, and found the generally accepted names to be the names 5
of the substrata that belong to these elements mixed with others.
Whereupon he inquired about the species of the "elements" that
have generally accepted names, and whenever the local motion
of one of these species was close to being the local motion of a
certain element, or its sensible qualities close to being the
qualities of a certain element, he transferred to the sum of that
element the name of the corresponding species. He called the 10
body that is together with [that is, next to] the heavenly bodies,
Fire; and he made it known that it is not this fire that we have.
For *fire* is applied to flame and ember by the multitude, not to
anything else. But since the movement of flame, especially, is a
movement that aims, as it were, at burning air in order to
ascend above it, he therefore called the body floating over the rest
of the elements (that is, that which has one of its two sur- 15
faces contiguous to the concave of the heavenly bodies) by the
name *Fire*.[1] He called the body that is below it by the name *Air,*
that which is below it by the name *Water,* and that which is
in the center by the name *Earth*. All the elements are associated
in the body that is in the center, that is, earth; that is required
theoretically and is evident by observation. Since mixture is of
two types, *Earth* is mixed with the rest of the elements according 20
to both of the two types. *Water* also is mixed with *Earth* and *Air*
in both ways; its mixture with *Fire* is not noticeable, however;
yet it is required that it be mixed with it also. *Air* is inferior to
Water in this respect, and *Fire* is inferior to them all in its
mixture with the others. These, then, are things of which he
made an exhaustive investigation.

60 Then afterwards he investigated their primary mixtures **107**
(in which neither of the two mixed elements abandons its essence),
and he investigated the species of such mixtures. Since the mix-

tures from them are almost infinite, he did not find names for
them, not even for the ones that are evidently distinct from each
other, except for a few of their species, such as *vapor, smoke,
flame,* and the like.   5

ix

61   When he was forced to find names for many of them,
he had to call each by the name of the element that predominates
in its essence: thus that in which *Air* predominates, he called
aerial; that in which *Fire* predominates he called *fiery;* that in   10
which *Earth* predominates he called *earthy;* and that in which
Water predominates he called *watery.* He went on to distinguish
the different names for them by means of the *differentia* inherent
in them: some, by means of their local motions, and others by
means of their sensible qualities; where two of these associate in
combination, he combined the names, such as *watery-earthy* and
the like.

62   Then, after this, he investigated the attributes and affec-   15
tions engendered in these four bodies whose condition he had
stated. He gave an account of their essences and material con-
stituents that admit those affections; and he made known their
agent causes and principles: those that exist in the element
together with the heavenly bodies, those in air, those in water, and
those in earth.

63   Then he investigated whether these elements exist for   20
the sake of themselves because they are among the things by   **108**
which the being is rendered perfect; or whether they were made
in order that the other generated bodies be produced from them;
or for the two things together, so that they are everlasting because they are parts of the beings and complete the whole, and
are concomitantly elements whose combination with each other
gives rise to all generated bodies. He investigated also whether   5
or not the attributes and affections generated in them are intended
directly for certain purposes and ends, or follow as consequences
and concomitants of things that in turn are engendered for certain purposes, or are only excesses and infirmities that do not

follow as consequences of a purpose or for the prevention of a purpose, so that their excess is like having an additional finger on the hand, while their lack is like being deprived of a finger.   10

All these things are to be found in a book he called *Meteorology*, especially in the [first] three treatises of this book.[1]

64   Then afterwards he set out to conduct a general inquiry into the bodies that originate in the combination of these four elements with each other. In general, the bodies that originate   15 from their combination are of two types: the one is the homogeneous, the other the heterogeneous. Heterogeneous bodies originate only from that combination of homogeneous bodies in which the essence of every one of the latter bodies is preserved: it is the combination of being together and in contact. As to the homogeneous bodies, they originate only from that combination in which the essence of every one of the parts is not preserved   20 in the way explained by him previously: it is rather the combination in which the parts blend together as a result of acting on each other and being acted on by each other. In turn, homogeneous bodies are of two types: those that only form parts of a heterogeneous body, and those every one of which is generated to   **109** form a part of nothing other than the sum of the world, the sum of the generated bodies, or the sum of a certain genus or species.

First, he began to investigate how the homogeneous bodies are generated from the elements; how an element associates with another; and which of the combined elements functions as the agent,   5 other; and which of the combined elements functions as the agent, by which of their powers some elements come to function as the material, by which power some of them function as the agent, and which of the qualities in them lead to their generation. He also summed up these same ideas regarding their corruption. And he explained the kinds of affection that lead to their generation, the   10 kinds of affection that lead to their corruption, and the place where this occurs. From his previous arguments, it became evident to him that the place must be the center and what is next to the center of the earth, inside it, and on its surface.

65   Then he set out to enumerate the tactile qualities present in homogeneous bodies and in the combined parts that adhere to   15 the primary powers because of which the elements act on each other and are acted on by each other, and because of which some ele-

ments admit action and other elements act on what admits action. He closely investigated the tactile qualities whose existence in the compound body adheres to the active powers of the elements, and the ones that adhere to the powers in virtue of which bodies come   20 to be acted on.

66   Then he intended to investigate all the particular qualities perceived by the other senses. However, it seemed to him, or rather he was of the opinion, that in many of them it is not sufficient to consider them as reflections of the powers because of **110** which the elements act on each other; no, they require other powers of the elements or powers that proceed from the actions of other bodies. Therefore it seemed to him that he should postpone the inquiry into them to another place in natural science: that is, the place where one investigates sense-perception as integrated with sight, with hearing, or with the other senses; for colors require   5 rays in order to exist and, with the exception of the tactiles, the other sensibles require air and water.[1]

All these things are to be found in the fourth treatise of the book that he called *Meteorology*.

67   Then he followed this by the inquiry into the homog-   10 eneous bodies that are generated from the elements and that are not parts of heterogeneous bodies: that is, stones, bodies consisting of stone, and the like. He investigated in this connection the earth and its parts and the classes of common vapors. Among the latter, he distinguished what is fiery, what is aerial, what is watery, and   15 what is mixed with many things belonging to the parts of earth; and the hot vapors among which some incline, further, more to dryness, some incline more to moisture, some are clearer and thinner, and some possess more smokiness. (It seems that these are the vapors that join themselves to the *internal* heat that ripens the bodies inside the earth and on its surface, and are mixed of water and earth or of the moist and the dry, the sum of which is what   20 admits being acted on by the hot and the cold—the two agent powers of the homogeneous bodies.) He explained that the primary causes for the generation of these different vapors inside the earth are, first, the heavenly bodies, and next, the air that chances **111** to be together with the earth and is heated or cooled by the heavenly bodies.

68   Then afterwards he set out to explain the classes of what inheres in every mixed earthy part and thus gives rise to the various types of stony and mineral bodies in the depth of the earth   5 and on its surface. He had to enumerate here such species of them as have been observed and such attributes as have been observed to exist in them and in each of their species. Once these were distinguished from each other, he proceeded to give an account of the essence of each of their materials and forms, and to give an account of the agent principles of each of these things or of the principles that act on the essences of their attributes, the agent principles of   10 each one of these attributes, and the ends for the sake of which each one of them is generated. However, since it is not easy to give an account of the ends unless one knows beforehand the end of the totality of the world, he postponed the inquiry into their ends to the science in which he would investigate the ultimate principles of the world.

All this is to be found in a book of his that he called *On Minerals*.[1]

69   Then afterwards he proceeded to inquire into the hetero-   15 geneous natural bodies. He began with the plants before the animals. First, he enumerated what is known about them by sense-perception and observation. He enumerated each species. He enumerated what can be observed from the enumeration of every species, and the attributes that can be observed in each species and   20 in each part of every species, until he exhausted all of them or whatever was available and known to him.

70   Then, after that, he proceeded to state the end for the sake   **112** of which each organ of every species of plants is generated.

71   Then, after that, he investigated the generation of each species of plants. He gave in every one an account of the material from which it is generated and the agent through which it is gen-   5 erated, until he exhausted everything natural about plants. He did the same regarding the attributes that exist in each.[1]

72   Then, after that, he proceeded to inquire about animals. First, he took what can be known about animals by observation and sense-perception. He enumerated the species of animals, or the ones known to him.

73   Then he enumerated the organs of each species. He   10

explained, regarding every species, of how many organs it is composed. He enumerated what can be observed about each organ. And he enumerated also what can be observed about the attributes of each species of animals, and the acts that each species performs in the things it manipulates.

x

74   When he had exhausted all of this, he suddenly saw that   15
nature and natural principles are not sufficient in most matters relating to animals and in many matters relating to plants; no, in addition to nature and the natural principles, one requires another principle and other powers of the same kind as this other principle; this principle should have the same place in animals and in many things belonging to plants as nature in natural beings. Thus while   **113**
in many things belonging to animals he had to give an account of their principles based on nature, in many other things the account of their principles had to be based on this other principle. He called this other principle the *soul*. He stated that plants are plants by virtue of the soul, and animals are animals by virtue of the soul. He called the principles that are of the same kind as the soul, the *animate* [or *psychical*] principles and powers.

First he began to investigate everything that belongs to animals   5
by nature (for he had previously summed up what nature is and what natural principles are), and to give an account of all that belongs to animals by nature. He investigated first the natural ends for the sake of which every organ of every species of animal is generated by nature. In every one of them, he gave an account of the nature that admits its essence: that is, the materials from which every species of animal is generated. He made known the   10
natural agent principle of every species of animal. And in every one of them he gave an account of the nature in virtue of which it is a natural substance, and of the end for the sake of which all that belongs to it by nature is generated.

It became evident to him from this that natural bodies are of two types. The first is the type rendered substantial to the utmost   15
by the nature that is the *essence* of each natural substance. The

second is the type rendered substantial by nature in order that
its substance (that is, its nature in act) be a beginning—in the
way of preparation and matter, or in the way of instrument—for
another principle, which is thus related to nature as the natural
form is related to its material or to the powers that are its instrument. This other principle is the soul.[1]   20

xi   114

75   When he had come to know this, then he had to investigate what the soul is, just as he had investigated previously what
nature is; and he had to know the psychical powers and the acts
generated from the soul, just as he did with regard to nature. He   5
proceeded to do so with the intention of knowing *what* the soul is,
and *by what* and *how* it is. He investigated whether it is many or
one—if it is many, in what way is it many: does it have many parts
or many powers? and if it has many parts, in what way are its parts
many: are they in many places, materials, and bodies dispersed in   10
many places? are they many in the manner in which the parts of the
same ˙homogeneous or heterogeneous body are many? or are its
parts many in another manner?—and what are the powers and principles of the soul.

He began to investigate what the soul in general is, just as
he investigated what nature is. He explained that the essence
of the *animate* natural substance is constituted by the soul, just as   15
the essence of the natural substance is constituted by nature; the
soul is that by which the animate substance—I mean that which
admits of life—is realized as substance; and the soul, like nature,
combines three aspects of being a principle: it is a principle as
an agent, it is a principle as a form, and it is a principle as an end.
All that was said of nature as a principle and as a substance ought   20
to be transferred to the soul. But as to whether the soul is a
substance as a material, there is some doubt that has not as yet
been clarified. For in the case of nature, it had become evident
that it is a principle in all four respects; and now it has become
evident that that nature which is the essence by which substance   **115**

is first realized as a bodily substance in act is also the material
of the soul.

76   Then he made known the animate powers in the same way
in which he had made it known that the natural powers by which
nature acts, and the natural bodies whose action is by nature, are   5
instruments of nature. Just as there may be a certain nature that
is an instrument of nature, a nature that is subservient to another
nature, and a ruling nature using the nature that is either subservient or an instrument, there may likewise be a ruling soul and
another soul that is either subservient or an instrument. There
are thus two types of natural bodies: a type rendered entirely substantial by nature, and a type not rendered substantial by nature,   10
but prepared by nature as a material or instrument for the soul.
That by which the latter is rendered substantial, after having been
rendered substantial by nature, will be the soul. The natural
substance that admits of soul will thus be the material of the soul;
and nature will be either a preparation, a material, or an instrument to be used by the soul in its acts. Thus there will be two types
of nature in animate substances: a type that is a material, and a
type that is an instrument. Hence in the animate substances nature   15
is not for its own sake but for the sake of the soul.

Therefore, just as he distinguished in natural things between
the nature that rules and the nature that is either subservient
or an instrument, he distinguished likewise among all of these
in the soul. And just as he made known the actions generated
from nature, and the attributes that adhere to the natural substances and are generated in them from nature, likewise he made
known the acts generated from the soul and the attributes that   20
exist in animate substances—insofar as they are animate—and are
generated in them from the soul. Since some of the attributes generated in natural substances are in them on account of their
materials and others on account of their forms, the attributes in   **116**
animate substances are divided likewise in the same way: some
of them exist in animate substances—insofar as they are animate
—on account of their specific materials and others adhere to
them on account of their form, that is, the soul.

Therefore he began to investigate first the most prior act of the   5

soul: that is, nutrition and what follows nutrition. He investigated in virtue of which power and part of the soul nutrition takes place, and he distinguished between that which rules and that which is instrument and subservient in this respect. He investigated the natural bodily instruments employed by this soul or this power in its actions. He investigated the natural instruments, e.g.,   10
heat and cold, employed by this soul in its actions. He investigated its acts, of how many species they are, what each of them is, of what it is composed, for what each act is utilized, and how each organ ought to be if it is to be utilized in each one of the acts of this soul by each of the species of animals.

77   Then he investigated the nourishment on which this soul   15
or this animate power acts, and how it receives some of it from the first elements themselves (because of what nature—that is, the elements—prepared with the assistance of the heavenly bodies), and the rest from other things beyond the elements. He explained by what plants are nourished and by what animals are nourished; and that, of the animals, some eat each other, others eat the plants,   20
others eat what is similar to that by which plants are nourished, and still other animals combine all or most of this nourishment.

78   Then he investigated whether the species of bodies that   **117**
have become nourishments are at the outset made by nature for the nourishment of animals and plants; or whether such bodies are generated for their own sake as parts of the world, but as they become suitable for the nourishment of animals and plants they are used as nourishment merely because they happen to be suitable, or whether it is not by chance that these things are nourishments   5
for animals and plants; or whether their generation for their own sake or as a part of the world is such that their perfection and purpose consists in their being for the sake of the things nourished by them. He investigated closely; for this investigation of these things is similar to the preceding investigation of whether the elements are for their own sake or for the generation of other bodies.

At first he made an imperfect investigation here of these things.   10
For it was denied him to go beyond this in the study of the world. Hence he abandoned them and proceeded to other things.[1]

He investigated health and disease and the species of each.

He proceeded to look into each of the species of health and of
disease: what causes its occurrence, for what and in what thing   15
it occurs, and from what it occurs. For health and disease inhere
in the animate substance because of their nature and natural
powers, which pertain specifically to what is animate. Therefore
one may consider their primary principle to be the soul. For the
soul itself is the cause (as the end and, with the help it receives
from nature, as the agent) of having this specific material present
in the soul. And nature, and the specific difference by which the   20
material has been prepared, and the natural powers that *now*
belong to that nature by which the material is prepared for the
specific difference, all belong to a thing possessing a soul. It is **118**
in this way, then, that all these are referred to the soul as both
their agent principle and their end.

That is to be found in his book *On Health and Disease.*[2]

79   Then he investigated the transformation of animals from   5
one age to another, which inheres in the animate substance because
of its specific nature.

80   Then he investigated each of the ages of the animate
substance and the attributes that, in each of its ages, inhere in it
because of the specific nature and natural powers of the animate
substances.

That is to be found in his book *On Youth and Old Age.*

81   Then he investigated the long life of the species of ani-   10
mals that are long-lived, or the short life of those of their species
that are short-lived. He investigated its causes and its natural and
animate principles.[1]

82   Then, after that, he investigated life and death: what each
of them is (that is, the continuous existence and the corruption
of animals with respect to their soul), and from what, in what, and   15
for the sake of what it takes place.

All these acts and attributes proceed from a soul or an animate
power similar to nature and close to it in its substance and essence,
but which is not nature. For it is present both in plants and in
animals, and plants are as it were intermediate between animals
and stony bodies. (There are some who are uncertain whether **119**
plants belong to animate or to natural things, and many tend to

attach them to the animals.) Therefore this soul, or this particular power of the soul, is close to nature.[1]

83   Then, after that, he investigated sense-perception (and the senses) as a part of a soul or of an animate power. He inves-   5
tigated the states of each of the senses, and the subjects on which the senses act—that is, the sensibles: what each of them is, how many species each of them has, what each of its species is, and in what, from what, and for the sake of what it is.

84   Then he investigated closely the natural organs in which these senses are and by which they sense (some of these organs are   10
the materials of the senses and others their instruments): how the nature of each of those organs ought to be, and what natural powers and attributes ought to be in each. He studied by induction every organ in which the senses and their acts reside. And he gave an account of the causes of what resides in them based on this part or this power of the soul.   15

That is to be found in a book of his that he called *On Sense and the Sensible*.

85   Then, after that, he investigated the classes of local motions that result from the soul in the bodies that breathe: what they are, the character of each of their species, by means of   20
which instruments and organs they take place, and through which power of the soul they take place, just as he had investigated the local motions that result in natural bodies from nature. He enumerated the organs equipped for such motion in every species   **120**
of animals. He gave an account of the principles (whether a nature, natural powers, or natural attributes) of all the things present in each of these organs, and he gave an account of their causes and principles in respect of these powers or this part of the soul. These motions are the ones by which animals labor in the pursuit of a thing or in flight from a thing.   5

It is at this point that he had to investigate the localities of animals and the localities of each species of animals, for what animals need a locality, and what the locality suitable to each animal is. For in some localities animals labor in the pursuit of their nourishment; in others animals take refuge to keep themselves safe at the times and under the conditions in which they   10
cannot or need not labor, or to keep themselves safe against an

enemy; and in still others they keep their offspring and rear them. Many animals require localities for the safekeeping of their nourishment; these are the animals that have to keep provisions for a long time to come, for some keep their provisions while others acquire their nourishment day by day.

That is to be found in his book *On the Local Motions of*   15 Animals.[1]

86   Then, after that, he investigated what respiration is, by means of which organs it takes place, how it takes place, and for the sake of what and through which power of the soul it takes place.[1]

87   Then, after that, he investigated what sleep and waking and dream-vision are, in what they take place, how they take place,   20 and for what reason and because of which power of the soul they take place.[1] He investigated the classes of dreams and dream-visions, and their causes and principles.[2]   **121**

He investigated the dreams that warn of future events, and he investigated the mode of interpreting dream-visions.[3] But the investigation here made him stop short, because he saw that neither the soul alone, nor the soul together with natural powers, is sufficient to explain the dream-vision that warns of future events. This requires other principles with a rank of being higher than   5 that of the soul. Therefore he postponed its investigation and exhaustive treatment.[4]

88   Then he examined memory, remembering, forgetting, and recollection: what each of them is, how it takes place, and in virtue of which power of the soul it takes place.[1]

He investigated also the faculty of the soul that produces the   10 cognitions that belong to the classes of animals devoid of intellect, and he summed up these cognitions and made known that for the sake of which they are.[2]

xii

89   When he investigated these things insofar as they are common to the species of animals other than man, he confined himself to giving an account of their principles and causes on the basis of the soul and the animate powers.[1]   15

xiii

90 When he investigated these identical things in man, he
saw that in man the soul alone is not sufficient for giving an account
of their causes. For observation shows that in man these things **122**
are an equipment for acts that go beyond, and are more powerful
than, the acts of the soul. He found in man other things not present
in the rest of the animals, whose causes and principles cannot
be either the soul or the animate powers, or nature or the natural   5
powers. Were one to examine the nature and the natural powers
that are in man, he would find them equipped for acts that go beyond, and are higher than, the acts of nature and the acts of the
soul. Were one to examine the soul and the animate powers in
man, he would find them insufficient for rendering man in the highest degree substantial. He was therefore forced at this point to investigate for what these other things are made. He found man with
speech, and speech proceeds from the intellect or the intellectual   10
principles and powers.

Therefore he was forced to investigate what the intellect[1] is
(just as he had investigated what the soul is and what nature is),
whether the intellect is indivisible or divisible like the soul, and
whether it has parts or powers. It became evident to him that the   15
intellect is like the soul and nature; the intellect is divisible into
parts or into powers; it is a principle underlying the essence of
man; it is also an agent principle; it is a cause and a principle as
an end like nature; and the intellect and the intellectual powers
are to the soul and the animate powers as the soul and the animate
powers are to nature and the natural powers. Just as natural sub-   20
stances were of two types—one rendered entirely substantial by
nature and another that nature renders substantial as an equipment (a material or an instrument) for the soul—the animate **123**
substances are likewise of two types: one rendered entirely substantial by the soul and another that the soul renders substantial
as material or instrument for the intellect and the intellectual
powers. He investigated whether the intellect is divisible like the
soul and nature into a ruling part and a subservient part. And he   5
investigated which intellectual power is for which, and whether
the intellect is for the soul and nature, or whether both nature and
the soul are for the intellect.

Therefore he had to investigate the acts of the intellectual
power and the acts of the intellect in general. Everything whose
substance is not identical with its act is not generated for its own   10
essence but for its act. It has become evident [from the study of
nature and the soul] that the intellect in virtue of which man is
finally rendered substantial is an intellect in its first perfection.
Now what is in its first perfection is still in potentiality, and the
potential is generated for its act; and this is precisely the thing
whose substance is not identical with its act.

xiv   15

91   When he investigated the acts of the intellectual powers
and the acts of the intellect, he found that all of their acts consist in rendering the beings intelligible to the intellect. However,
he found that some intelligibles are perceived only to the extent
that enables man to bring them into actual existence outside the
intellect in natural things;[1] there are others that cannot be brought   20
into actual existence by man in natural things; and of some of those
that can be made to exist, the intellect has a kind of perception that
exceeds the measure required and useful for their existence. He   **124**
called the intellectual faculty that perceives the beings that can be
brought into actual existence in natural things by man—provided
he has that kind of intellectual perception of them that is useful to
him in making them exist—the *practical* intellect; and the faculty
that perceives the intelligibles in a manner not useful to man in the
sense that he can make any of them exist in natural things, the
theoretical intellect.[2] And he called the intellectual faculty by   5
which what has been acquired by the practical intellect can be
made to exist in natural things, *volition* and *choice*.[3]

xv

92   When he investigated the last two intellectual faculties,
he found that they are subordinate faculties with subservient acts.
He investigated the things in which they serve. He found that   10
they serve primarily natural and psychical things belonging to man;

however, they are not things that can exist in man for their own
sake, but only so that he may attain intellectual perfection. He
investigated the intellect for which such natural and psychical
things have been provided at the outset, whether they are for   15
the sake of that part of the intellect [that is, volition and choice]
that serves them, or whether the intellect serves them in this
manner only to serve something else or a certain intellect other
than the subordinate part. He investigated whether the subordinate
part performs its service having its own essence as the end, or
the things that it serves. It became evident to him that it is not
possible that its end be those things that it serves; no, these are
used only as materials or instruments, while it itself rules and   20
uses them. He investigated whether its rulership is such that it
could not serve anything else. He found that all of its acts are   **125**
such that they need not serve anything else. Therefore it became
evident that if it exists merely for the sake of this kind of activity,
its nature—and its essence and substance—could not enjoy supreme
rule or be the highest.

Thus he investigated the theoretical part of the intellect. He
found that the intelligible acquired by this intellect are intelligibles   5
with which it cannot at all serve something else; and he found
that, when this intellect is realized in its final perfection, it will be
realized as an intellect in act after having been potential. Therefore he laid down that it had been realized in act and that it had
acquired the intelligibles. He investigated in what way and in
what mode it acquires the theoretical intelligibles as intelligibles
in act. He laid down that they may be acquired in the highest
possible degree, and that it may acquire its final perfection be-   10
ond which no further perfection can be acquired. Therefore he
found that, when it is such, its substance is identical with its act
or comes close to being its act.

xvi

93 When he had found this to be the case, and that the
intellect could not enjoy another existence more perfect than this   15
one that renders it entirely substantial, he realized that this is

the final thing that renders man substantial, and that when the substance of man is realized in that final perfection beyond which it
is impossible that there be further perfection, the substance of this
part comes close to being identical with its act. It follows as a
consequence from this that the ends pursued by the intellectual
faculties, whenever they serve anything, are pursued for the realization of this part of the intellect, which is the theoretical intellect.   20
This intellect is the substance of man. If at the outset his substance   **126**
is not identical with his act, and it becomes so only through the
intellect when the substance of the intellect comes close to being
its act, it follows as a consequence that the other faculties—that is,
the practical intellectual faculties—have been realized only for the
sake of this part, and that the soul and nature were made only
so that this part of the intellect be realized, first in potentiality,   5
and subsequently in its final perfection and most completely.

94   Then, after that, he investigated whether it is possible that
nature and the soul be sufficient for reaching this perfection. He
explained that nature and the soul cannot be sufficient for man to
reach this perfection, but that he needs the two practical intellectual faculties [that is, volition and choice] in addition to the
soul and nature and their acts.

xvii   10

95   When he had finally inquired into this matter, he turned
once again to the things he had investigated with reference to what
man is by nature and what exists in man because of the soul:[1] he
gave an account of their causes based on these intellectual faculties,
since those things are provided—either as material or as instrument—so that the practical intellectual faculties can employ them   15
in order to realize the theoretical intellect in the most perfect way
in which this is possible.

96   Then he investigated whether the animate substances
other than man exist for utilization by the practical faculties in
perfecting what man is by nature and what belongs to man because
of the soul and to equip both for attaining this perfection; and
whether those animate substances are *provided* for the sake of

these practical intellectual faculties, or whether this happens by   20
chance. This investigation is identical with the investigation
whether the elements are provided for the sake of all that is   **127**
generated from them, whether the natural substances are provided for the animate, and whether the animate substances are
provided for the intellect and the intellectual powers.[1]

xviii

97   When he investigated these matters, however, what he was
looking for became clear to him only in part; he encountered a   5
difficulty with respect to the rest because he had not yet pursued
another investigation. That is, what is acquired upon the perfection of the soul and its faculties, prior to the contribution made by
the practical faculties, is the potential intellect, and this potential
intellect is there on account of the service it renders to the intellectual faculties. Therefore he investigated whether the service
rendered by those two [that is, nature and the soul] is sufficient,
in the absence of another principle, to attain the perfection of the
theoretical intellect. It became evident that this is impossible and
that it is insufficient: the actual intellect requires something else.   10
This need is not only felt in respect of the theoretical intellect: the
practical[1] faculties too require other principles. For no intelligibles
could be acquired by the practical intellectual faculty or by the
theoretical faculty through volition and reflection, if these were
not already equipped with primary intelligibles, which are principles by nature used in acquiring these other intelligibles.

Therefore he had to investigate now whether these primary   15
intelligibles are eternally in the potential intellect. But how is this
possible when the potential intellect is not eternal? It follows then
that these primary intelligibles (which are in the potential intellect by nature and not by volition), did not exist at first, and that
subsequently the potential intellect came into perfect possession
of them. And it had become evident in general that the potential
cannot move to act except through an immediate agent of the
same species as the thing that is to be realized in act, from which   20
it follows necessarily that there is here a certain intellect, uncom-   **128**

pounded and in act, that has engendered the primary intelligibles
in the potential intellect and has equipped it by nature to receive
all the other intelligibles.

xix

98   When he investigated this intellect, he found that it is an
intellect in act, had never been potential, and has always been and   5
will always be (what has never been potential is not in a material,
its substance and act are identical or close to being identical);
when the human intellect achieves its ultimate perfection, its substance comes close to being the substance of this intellect. He
called this intellect the *Active Intellect.* And it became evident
to him that in achieving the perfection of its substance, the human intellect follows the example of this Intellect. This Intellect
is the end because its example is followed in this manner, it   10
is the most perfect end, and it is the agent. It is thus the principle of man as the agent, ultimately, of that which renders man
substantial insofar as he is man. It is the end because it is that
which gave him a principle with which to labor toward perfection and an example to follow in what he labors at, until he comes
as close to it as he possibly can. It is, then, his agent, it is his end,   15
and it is the perfection the substance of which man attempts to
approach. Hence, it is a principle in three respects: as an agent,   ·
as an end, and as the perfection that man attempts to approach.
It is therefore a separate form of man, a separate end and a prior
end, and a separate agent; in some manner, man becomes united
with it when it is intellected by him. And it became evident that
the thing whose very substance and nature are nothing but mind   20
can be intellected and can exist outside the intellect—there is no difference between these two modes of its existence. Hence it became
clear that it is intellected by man only when he is not separated   **129**
from it by an intermediary. In this way, the soul of man itself
becomes this Intellect. Since the human soul is for the sake of this
Intellect, the nature by which man acquires what is natural to him
is for the sake of the soul only, and the soul is for the sake of the
theoretical intellect in its highest perfection, it follows that all   5

these things belong to man so that he may attain this rank of being.

At this point Aristotle returned once again to investigate those matters that had escaped him,[1] in many of which he now detected the causes of the difficulties.

99   Then he investigated whether the Active Intellect is also the cause of the existence of nature and natural things and of the   10
soul and animate things. It had become evident to him that the heavenly bodies are the principles that move the elements and the other bodies.[1] Therefore he investigated whether the Intellect assists the heavenly bodies with respect to the existence of the beings encompassed by the heavenly bodies: that is, he had to investigate whether the heavenly bodies are sufficient for the beings to be realized, some possessing a nature, others possessing a soul,   15
and still others possessing an intellect. As for possessing an intellect in act, it had become evident that the heavenly bodies are not sufficient without the Active Intellect;[2] and it had become evident with respect to what acquires its perfection from the Active Intellect, that its movement is supplied by nature and the soul with the assistance of the heavenly bodies. Furthermore, many things possessing soul supply a soul to the materials they encounter,   20
provided these materials are equipped by nature to receive it: a man is begotten by a previous man, thus man is from man, and likewise most animals and most plants. (In the case of animals there are some that are not generated from animals, and some plants are not generated from plants; and minerals are not generated from others of the same species as they.)

Therefore he had to investigate these things. But he had to go   **130**
beyond this and investigate what at the outset supplied "humanity" in general, "donkeyness" in general, and the form of each species whose particular instances then came to be generated from each other; for what are generated are only the particular instances of each species.[3] He had, then, to investigate what supplied the form   5
of that species, and, more generally, what supplied the forms of the species, whether the heavenly bodies or the Active Intellect, or whether the Active Intellect supplied only the form and the heavenly bodies supplied the motions of the materials. For up till now it had not become evident that the heavenly bodies supplied the natural bodies with anything besides motion.

Therefore he had to investigate also whether the substances of
the heavenly bodies consist of a nature or a soul or an intellect,   10
or something else more perfect than these. These matters are
beyond the scope of natural theory. For natural theory includes
only what is included in the categories; and it has become evident
that there are here other instances of being not encompassed by
the categories: that is, the Active Intellect and the thing that supplies the heavenly bodies with perpetual circular motion.

Therefore he had to inquire into the beings in a way more   15
inclusive than natural theory. For his investigations in natural
science made it evident that, in the end, natural theory terminates
in the Active Intellect and the mover of the heavenly bodies, and
then stands still. Further, the sum of the preceding inquiry has led
to the conclusion that that nature which is in man, and the human
soul, the powers and the acts of these two, as well as the practical   20
intellectual powers, are all for the perfection of the theoretical intellect; and nature, the soul, and the psychical intellect[4] are insufficient without the acts generated from volition and choice, both of
which adhere to the practical intellect.

Therefore he had also to investigate the acts generated from   **131**
the will, volition, and choice, which adhere to the practical intellect
—for it is these that make up the *human* will. This is because
desire and the things adhering to sense-perception and discernment, which are possessed by other animals, are neither human
nor useful for achieving theoretical perfection; for no other animal   5
is equipped to achieve theoretical perfection. Therefore he had to
investigate all the acts generated from volition and choice. For
choice means the will that adheres to the practical intellect;
therefore comparable things in other animals are not called *choice*.

Therefore he had to inquire into, and to investigate, the acts   10
generated from these, and distinguish the acts useful for the ultimate purpose from those that obstruct the way to it. He had to
investigate also the natural things, whether instruments or a
material, useful in making up these acts. Hence he had to investigate also that nature which is useful for the animate substances of
animals and plants, and bring into existence[5] those of them that
contribute to the acts leading or proceeding to human perfection.   15
He had to investigate also the other natural beings—whether

stones, minerals, or elements—and bring into existence what is
useful; and likewise bring into existence also those useful things
among them that have the heavenly bodies as their causes, and
use them. However, how to use such things, and the different ways
in which to use them with respect to animals, plants, and so on is
open to discussion; indeed, were man to make a thorough investigation, he would find that it cannot be made evident either in
natural science or in human science without completing the inquiry   20
into, and the investigation of, the beings that are *above* things
natural in their rank of being.[6]

Therefore he had to give precedence to that inquiry in order
to achieve a more perfect knowledge of natural things and com-   **132**
plete the natural *philosophy*, and the political and human *philosophy*, which they lacked.[7]

Therefore Aristotle proceeded in a book that he called *Metaphysics*[8] to inquire into, and to investigate, the beings in a manner
different than natural inquiry.

*   *   *

It has become evident from the preceding that it is necessary
to investigate, and to inquire into, the intelligibles that cannot be
utilized for the soundness of human bodies and the soundness of   5
the senses; the understanding of the causes of visible things, which
the soul desired, is more human than that knowledge that was
construed to be the necessary knowledge.

It has become evident that that necessary knowledge is for the
sake of this understanding; the knowledge that of old we used to
suppose as superfluous is not, but is the *necessary* knowledge for
rendering man substantial or making him reach his final perfection.   10
And it has become evident that the knowledge that he [Aristotle]
investigated at the outset just because he loved to do so, and in-
spected for the sake of explaining the truth about the above-
mentioned pursuits, has turned out to be necessary for realizing the
political activity[9] for the sake of which man is made. The knowledge
that comes next is investigated for two purposes: one, to render
perfect the human activity[10] for the sake of which man is made,   15
and second, to perfect our defective natural science, for we do not   **133**
possess metaphysical science.

Therefore philosophy must necessarily come into being in
every man in the way possible for him.

Translator's
Notes

Part I: THE ATTAINMENT OF HAPPINESS

(1) 1. For a more elaborate statement on the distinction between "this" and the "other" life and the relation between them, see, e.g., Alfarabi, *Aphorisms of the Statesman* (*Fuṣūl al-madanī*), ed. and tr. D. M. Dunlop (Cambridge, 1961), secs. 25, 76; cf. *On the Intellect* (*Risālah fī al-ʿaql*), ed. Maurice Bouyges (Beyrouth, 1938), sec. 44.

2. Below, sec. 26.

3. Aristotle *Nicomachean Ethics* i. 13, vi. 1. 1138ᵇ35 ff., vi. 2–13, *Magna Moralia* i. 1. 1182ᵃ15 ff.; Alfarabi, *Statesman, secs.* 6–7, *Intellect,* secs. 9–11. For the transition from ethics to logic and the theory of demonstration, consider, e.g., Aristotle *Nicomachean Ethics* vi. 3 (*Posterior Analytics* i. 1).

(2) 1. See below, secs. 46 (where the theoretical virtues are again asserted to be sciences), 53 (38:19). Cf. Aristotle *Magna Moralia* i. 34. 1197ᵃ16–19.

2. For the two kinds of knowledge, see Aristotle *Posterior Analytics* i. 1, ii. 9, *Nicomachean Ethics* vi. 6; Alfarabi, *Intellect,* sec. 8.

3. These terms do not seem to be employed here in their technical sense. Alfarabi, *Logic* (*Manṭiq*), MS, Ḥamīdiyyah (Suleymania, Constantinople), No. 812, fol. 112r; Aristotle *Posterior Analytics* i. 33.

4. Below, III, sec. 3 (63:4–10).

(3) 1. Section 4, below, specifies four of these methods: the apodictic, sophistical, rhetorical, and poetic.

2. Alfarabi, *Enumeration of the Sciences* (*Iḥṣāʾ al-ʿulūm*), ed. Osman Amine (2nd ed.; Cairo, 1949), ch. 2 (53–58).

(4) 1. Alfarabi says: "all these methods are *technical* [in character] (*ṣināʿiyyah*)."

2. Alfarabi, *Enumeration of the Sciences,* ch. 2 (58–60).

3. Below, II, secs. 7–12, III, secs. 3 (70:15 ff.)–16; cf. Aristotle *Topics* i. 1.

(5) 1. For the source of the distinction between the "principle of instruction" and the "principle of being," between "what is better known to us" and "what is better known by nature," or between the *causa cognoscendi* and the *causa essendi*, consider Aristotle *Physics* i. 1. 184ᵃ16–23, i. 5. 189ᵃ4 (cf. *Posterior Analytics* i. 2. 71ᵇ34–72ᵃ6), *Nicomachean Ethics* i. 4. 1095ᵃ30 ff., vi. 3. 1139ᵇ25 ff. Alfarabi, *Logic,* fols. 76v–77r; below, III, secs. 7, 17.

2. Aristotle *Posterior Analytics* i. 2, 7, 9.

3. See below, sec. 6.

4. Aristotle *Posterior Analytics* i. 13, ii. 1–2; Alfarabi, *Logic*, fols. 62*v*–63*r*, 94*r*. Below, secs. 8, 11, 15.

(6)   1. These are the four ways of interpreting and asking the question *why* (above, sec. 5). Aristotle *Posterior Analytics* ii. 8–11, *Metaphysics* i. 3, v. 2, *Physics* ii. 3, 7. Below, III, sec. 7.

2. I.e., in what form or shape or state. Alfarabi, *Logic*, fol. 94.

3. Cf. Aristotle's enumeration of the causes in *Posterior Analytics* ii. 11. 94ᵃ20–23. It is perhaps of some importance that Alfarabi first presents a tripartite division and then states that the central question signifies *both* the material and efficient causes.

4. These are the first two meanings of *from* (or *out of*) enumerated by Aristotle in *Metaphysics* v. 24, cf. v. 2.

5. Cf. Aristotle *Metaphysics* xii. i. 1069ᵃ30 ff.

6. Below, secs. 11 ff.

(7)   1. Aristotle *Posterior Analytics* i. 28. 87ᵃ38–ᵇ4, *Metaphysics* iii. 1 ff., iv. 2.

2. Cf. above, sec. 6, below, sec. 11. The emphasis here seems to be on the fact that one may *find* only "two" principles. Cf. Aristotle *Physics* i. 6.

3. For examples of this procedure, see below, III, secs. 66, 74, 78, 90, 95, 98.

(8)   1. I.e., the principles of being.

2. Cf. Aristotle *Posterior Analytics* i. 2. 71ᵇ21–23. Above, sec. 5.

(10) 1. Cf. Aristotle *Nicomachean Ethics* vi. 8. 1142ᵃ12–19, *Posterior Analytics* i. 12. 77ᵇ27–33.

2. "Magnitude" is used here in the wider sense, including both discrete quantity (numbers) and continuous quantity (lines, surfaces, bodies). The "other" magnitudes (or quantities) thus means the continuous. In what follows Alfarabi uses "magnitude" to mean continuous quantity only, including (*a*) commensurable and (*b*) incommensurable magnitudes. Cf. Aristotle *Posterior Analytics* i. 7. 75ᵇ4, *Categories* ch. 6, *Metaphysics* v. 13. 1020ᵃ11.

3. I.e., beyond arithmetic and geometry.

4. Arithmetic, geometry, and the five disciplines mentioned here make up the seven broad divisions of mathematics. For a more detailed account of each, see Alfarabi, *Enumeration of the Sciences*, ch. 3.

(11) 1. Aristotle *Metaphysics* vi. 1. 1026ᵃ8–9, xi. 3. 1061ᵃ28 ff., *De Anima* iii. 8. 431ᵇ15, *Physics* ii. 2. 193ᵇ25 ff.

(12) 1. Alfarabi, *Statesman*, sec. 89, reproduces certain phrases and sentences scattered here in secs. 12–20.

2. Aristotle *Metaphysics* iii. 1. 995ᵇ15–18, iii. 2. 997ᵃ34–998ᵃ19.

(13) 1. Cf. Aristotle *Metaphysics* i. 3. 983ᵇ6 ff.

2. "Particular" or "individual" (*juzʾī, merikos*) is normally used in contrast to "whole" or "universal" (*kullī, holikos*). Alfarabi uses it to characterize the beings whose existence and knowledge involve a material constituent (in contrast to mathematical forms and incorporeal principles, cf. above, sec. 12, below, secs. 16, 19). They comprise natural things and the things of the will. He speaks of their "intelligibles" ("intelligible idea" [*maʿnā maʿqūl*]), which are "one in the species or the genus," and the "particular" or "individual" instances of them, which have, or can be brought into, actual existence outside the mind. See, below, secs. 22–26, 34, 38, III, secs. 52–53, 91, 99.

(14) 1. See below, III, secs. 17 ff.

(15) 1. Above, sec. 5 n. 1.

2. Cf. above, secs. 8–9.

(16) 1. See below, III, secs. 31 ff.

(17) 1. See the transition below, III, secs. 68–69.

2. Cf. below, III, secs. 69 ff.

(18) 1. Alfarabi's *Statesman*, sec. 89 (166:7), and, below, III, sec. 99, may support emending this phrase to read: "different from the physical [or natural]." In any event, at the end of the preceding section and in what follows the "genus of things" in question is stated: the "rational principles" with which man labors toward his perfection. "Different from the metaphysical" could mean: understood as principles of "political science" (below, sec. 20) rather than of "divine science" (below, sec. 19), or of the "practical" rather than the "theoretical" intellect (below, III, sec. 99).

2. See below, III, secs. 91 ff.

3. Cf. Alfarabi, *Virtuous City* (*al-Madīnah al-fāḍilah*), ed. Fr. Dieterici (Leiden, 1895), p. 53, *Political Regime* (*al-Siyāsah al-madaniyyah*) (Hyderabad, 1346 A.H.), pp. 38–39.

4. Below, sec. 20.

(19) 1. Sections 4 ff.

2. Alfarabi, following Aristotle, calls the inquiry into metaphysical things "divine inquiry" or theology. Contrary to our expectations, however, Alfarabi does not derive "divine" from God (*Allāh*) as in his more popular *Enumeration of the Sciences* (ch. 4 [100]), but from "the god" (*al-ilāh*). Cf., also, his *Purpose of Aristotle's "Metaphysics"* (*Gharaḍ Arisṭūṭālīs fī kitāb mā baʿd al-ṭabīʿah*) in *Alfārābī's philosophische Abhandlurgen*, ed. Fr. Dieterici (Leiden, 1890), pp. 34–38.

(20) 1. Alfarabi, *Virtuous City*, p. 46.

2. I.e., the "theoretical" part of it. Cf. below, sec. 26; Alfarabi, *Enumeration of the Sciences*, ch. 5 (103–4).

3. Alfarabi says "first principle" and "principles" respectively;
cf. the physical-metaphysical and political connotations of
archē (*archōn*): *principium-princeps*, "principle"-"prince."

4. Cf. Plato *Statesman* 274B ff.; below, III, sec. 3 (68:7–18).
Alfarabi, *Virtuous Religion* (*al-Millah al-fāḍilah*), MS, Leiden,
No. 1002, fols. 59*v*–60*v*, *Political Regime*, p. 54. As to the
character and ground of the correspondence between the city
and the world, see below, sec. 55.

(21) 1. Cf. above, secs. 17–20, below, secs. 22–26. According to this
account, the theoretical sciences include a "theoretical" human
or political science whose objects are the "intelligibles" or
"ideas" of voluntary things as distinct from their *actual* existence at particular times and places. Contrast Aristotle *Nicomachean Ethics* i. 5–6, vi. 3, 5 (cf., however, x. 9. 1180ᵇ14 ff.).

(22) 1. In this and the following sections Alfarabi elaborates his "solu-
tion" of the difficulties raised by Aristotle (*Nicomachean
Ethics* i. 6) against the Platonic "ideas."

(23) 1. Aristotle *Metaphysics* v. 6. 1016ᵇ31 ff.

2. The distinction between "natural" and "voluntary" intelligibles
and the meaning of "voluntary" intelligibles are stated below,
secs. 24 ff.

(24) 1. Aristotle *Nicomachean Ethics* iii. 3, vi. 4. 1140ᵃ14–15.

2. Aristotle *Nicomachean Ethics* iii. 1. 1110ᵇ16 ff., iii. 3.

3. Hence, the distinction between "man himself" and a particular
man, and so on, is meaningful. Contrast Aristotle *Nicomachean
Ethics* i. 6. 1096ᵃ34 ff.

(26) 1. Aristotle *Posterior Analytics* i. 6, 9.

2. Aristotle *Nicomachean Ethics* iii. 3, 5, vi. 1. 1138ᵇ35 ff., vi. 9.
The "rationative," "thinking," "calculative," or "reflective"
faculty (*fikriyyah*). Alfarabi defines it also (*Statesman*, sec. 6)
as "that by which we deliberate on the thing which we wish to
do, when we wish to know whether to do it is possible or not,
and if it is possible, how we must do the action." (Dunlop)
Cf. Alfarabi, *Intellect*, secs. 2–6.

(27) 1. Aristotle *Nicomachean Ethics* vi. 5. 1140ᵇ16–17, vi. 9.
1142ᵇ18 ff.

2. Aristotle *Nicomachean Ethics* iii. 4–5.

3. Alfarabi, *Statesman*, sec. 90 (168:5–6), *Intellect*, secs. 3–4,
reproduce part of this sentence; cf. Alfarabi, *Statesman*, sec.
88 (164:5–7).

(28) 1. Cf. above, sec. 25. Parts of this sentence and others in this
section are reproduced in Alfarabi, *Statesman*, sec. 90
(168:1–5).

2. Contrast Aristotle's description of the relation between "legislative wisdom" and what is "known by the general name 'po-

litical wisdom'" in *Nicomachean Ethics* vi. 8. 1141ᵇ23–26
(cf., however, x. 9. 1181ᵃ25–ᵇ1).
3. Aristotle *Nicomachean Ethics* vi. 8. 1141ᵇ27–28.
4. Aristotle *Nicomachean Ethics* vi. 8. 1141ᵇ29 ff.; Alfarabi,
Statesman, secs. 38, 41.
(29) 1. Aristotle *Nicomachean Ethics* vi. 5. 1140ᵇ16 ff., vi. 9. 1142ᵇ18–
23, vi. 12. 1144ᵃ6–36.
(31) 1. Cf. Aristotle *Nicomachean Ethics* i. 13, v. 1. 1129ᵇ25 ff.,
Magna Moralia i. 33.
(33) 1. "Generally accepted" opinions (*mashhūrāt*) are to be distinguished from "generally received" opinions (*maqbūlāt*).
The latter are based on the testimony of "one person or a
group acceptable to a particular person or group only."
Alfarabi, *Logic*, fol. 61v. Here, Alfarabi seems to substitute
"religion" (*millah*) for generally received opinions. Cf. below,
secs. 55 ff. In sec. 57 Alfarabi uses *mutaqabbal* ("well-
received") in relation to the *imam*.
2. *Millah* is a Koranic term, where it usually means religion. It
also designates the religious community or the congregation.
But it is clear from this section and secs. 55 ff. below that
Alfarabi is using *millah* here to designate the opinions and acts
of such a community. When he intends to designate the religious *community,* he speaks of the "followers of a particular
religion" (*ahl millatin mā*). Cf. Alfarabi, *Virtuous Religion,*
fol. 51v: "The *millah* consists of opinions and acts . . .
prescribed for a congregation by their supreme ruler."
3. "Everyone else" may mean (1) those who perform more particular functions, (2) those who wish to discover what is most
noble according to the followers of other religions, (3) those
who wish to discover what is most noble according to generally accepted opinion, or (4) those who wish to discover
what is truly most noble. For the relation between the deliberative and moral virtues in general, cf. above, secs. 29 ff.,
below, secs. 35 ff.
(34) 1. Contrast Aristotle's discussion of the relation between these
two faculties in *Nicomachean Ethics* vi. 5, 7.
(35) 1. Aristotle *Nicomachean Ethics* vi. 12.
2. I.e., "voluntary" as opposed to "natural"; cf. above, secs. 22 ff.,
below, III, sec. 3 (66:17).
3. Cf. Aristotle *Nicomachean Ethics* vi. 12. 1144ᵃ6 ff., vi. 13;
Alfarabi, *Harmonization of the Opinions of Plato and Aristotle*
(*al-Jamᶜ bayn raꜣyay al-ḥakīmayn Aflāṭūn al-ilāhī wa-Arisṭū-
ṭālīs*) in *Alfārābī's philosophische Abhandlungen*, ed. Fr.
Dieterici (Leiden, 1890), pp. 16:20–19:2.

(36) 1. Alfarabi, *Statesman*, sec. 9.
      2. Above, sec. 35.
(37) 1. Below, sec. 60.
      2. Cf. Alfarabi, *Political Regime*, pp. 44 ff., 49.
(38) 1. Cf. above, sec. 13 n. 2.
(39) 1. Aristotle *Nicomachean Ethics* ii. 1, x. 9. 1179ʰ20 ff.
      2. Alfarabi, *Political Regime*, pp. 43–44.
(40) 1. See below, sec. 57 (43:9–17).
      2. Sections 4 ff.
      3. *Ibid.*
      4. *Republic* ii. 376E–iv. 427C, vii. 521C–541B. Alfarabi, *Logic*, fol. 91r:4–5.
      5. This term (*bādiʾ al-raʾy al-mushtarak*) is an equivalent of "generally accepted opinion" (cf. above, sec. 33 n. 1) with the additional emphasis on its "unexamined" character. "The generally accepted opinions held by everyone *fī bādiʾ al-raʾy* . . . and *bādiʾ al-raʾy* is that which has not been scrutinized." Alfarabi, *Logic*, fol. 89v (cf. *Intellect*, secs. 7, 12). For the contrast between "unexamined" opinion and what is "subjected to thorough scrutiny," see below, secs. 50–51. This contrast indicates that the "examination" in question or "scrutiny" in question is not restricted to ascertaining whether the opinions are in fact generally held or only "appear" to be generally held "at first sight" (*fī ẓāhir al-ẓann*). Alfarabi, *Logic*, fol. 88v; Aristotle *De Sophisticis Elenchis* ch. 1.
      6. Cf. below, sec. 55 n. 1.
(41) 1. I.e., deliberative and moral.
      2. Aristotle *Nicomachean Ethics* x. 9. 1180ᵃ4 ff.
(42) 1. Aristotle *Nicomachean Ethics* x. 9. 1180ᵃ19 ff.; Plato *Statesman* 259C, *passim;* Alfarabi, *Plato's "Laws"* (*Nawāmīs Aflāṭūn*), ed. Fr. Gabrieli (London, 1952), II (12:1–2), III (20:1).
      2. Note, however, the end of the section and the following section where the dual aspect of this skill is emphasized.
(43) 1. Aristotle *Nicomachean Ethics* i. 9. 1099ᵇ32–10. 1100ᵃ20, x. 6. 1176ᵃ32, x. 8. 1178ᵇ24–27; Alfarabi, *Virtuous City*, p. 46. Cf. below, sec. 52.
      2. Alfarabi, *Political Regime*, p. 59:19 ff., *Virtuous City*, pp. 65–66.
      3. Alfarabi, *Plato's "Laws,"* IV (22:16 ff.), *Virtuous City*, pp. 60–61.
(44) 1. Sections 41–43, perhaps also secs. 28 ff.
      2. Aristotle *Rhetoric* i. 2, *passim.*
      3. Alfarabi, *Virtuous Religion*, fols. 53v–54v.
(45) 1. Alfarabi, *Political Regime*, pp. 40 ff.

2. Alfarabi, *Plato's "Laws,"* I (5:4–5), II (13:14–15:10, 16:12–19), *Political Regime,* pp. 46 ff.
3. The latter two sciences are (derivatively) "theoretical" (or "philosophic," cf. sec. 55 [40:12–13]) insofar as (*a*) they deal with opinions (vs. acts) and (*b*) their subjects were originally seized upon in the theoretical sciences properly so called (above, sec. 44, below, sec. 46). On the preservation of the law, cf. Alfarabi, *Plato's "Laws,"* VII.
(47) 1. Alfarabi, *Virtuous Religion,* fol. 54.
(48) 1. Alfarabi, *Political Regime,* pp. 48–49, 53–54.
(50) 1. Above, sec. 46.
       2. Above, sec. 40 n. 5; Alfarabi, *Political Regime,* pp. 55–56.
(51) 1. Or "follower," "successor" (*tābi*ᶜ). He functions as an "aide" or "subordinate" who is employed by the supreme ruler to apply and preserve his law (above, secs. 44, 47–48). In the absence of the supreme ruler, the "adherent" is envisaged as his "successor." This is a second-best arrangement; the ruler will then lack theoretical knowledge and hence the ability to be a true lawgiver (above, secs. 45 ff.). This rule "adheres to the supreme rule" (*ri*ᵃ*sah tābi*ᶜ*ah li-l-ūlā*) or takes it as a model. "He who assumes *this* office is called the *commander of the law* and the *prince of the law."* Alfarabi, *Virtuous Religion,* fol. 56r–v, cf. fol. 58r:20 ff., *Virtuous City,* pp. 60–61, 69–70, *Political Regime,* pp. 51, 54.
(52) 1. Above, sec. 46.
       2. Cf. Aristotle *Nicomachean Ethics* x. 7–8; above, secs. 1, 43, 45–46, 49. Consider, especially, the relation between sec. 43 and secs. 52 ff.
(53) 1. For an account of the "philosophic" sciences (mathematics, astronomy, and so on) of the "Chaldeans," cf., e.g., Ṣāᵈid al-Andalusī, *Classes of Nations* (*Ṭabaqāt al-umam*), ed. Louis Cheikho (Beirut, 1912), iv. 3.
       2. Southern Mesopotamia, the alluvial region bounded in the north by a line from al-Anbār to Takrīt. Cf. *ibid.* i.
       3. *Ibid.* iv. 6. Ṣāᵈid al-Andalusī reports the popular myth of the "prophetic" origin of the philosophic sciences. In addition to claiming that philosophy *alone* is true wisdom, Alfarabi insists (below, sec. 55 [41:12]) that "philosophy is prior to religion *in time."*
       4. *al-Siryān:* the Nestorian and Jacobite (Monophysite) Christians using Syriac as a literary medium in Syria, Mesopotamia, and the Persian Empire.
       5. Aristotle *Nicomachean Ethics* vi. 7. 1140ᵇ9–12. Below, III, secs. 7–9.
       6. BM, EH. "Human" H; "political" F. Cf. Aristotle *Nico-*

machean Ethics vi. 7. 1140ᵃ12–15 (wisdom "in general"), 1141ᵇ7 ff. ("practical," "human" wisdom).

 7. Cf. Aristotle *Nicomachean Ethics* vi. 7. 1141ᵇ16 ff.; Alfarabi, *Statesman*, sec. 34.

(54) 1. Contrast Aristotle *Nicomachean Ethics* vi. 7. 1140ᵇ20 ff. (and the reference to Anaxagoras and Thales in 1141ᵇ3 ff.), x. 8, x. 9. 1180ᵃ32 ff., 1180ᵇ14 ff. (cf., however, *Magna Moralia* i. 2. 1184ᵃ32 ff.). Alfarabi, *Harmonization of the Opinions of Plato and Aristotle*, pp. 4:21–5:21.

 2. Above, sec. 41 n. 1.

(55) 1. "Make comprehensible" (*tafhīm*) is apparently used as a synonym of "seizing upon the concept" (*taṣawwur*), the term employed usually in conjunction with "assent [to a proposition]" or "judgment" (*taṣdīq*). The sequel indicates, however, that "comprehension" and "assent" are employed by Alfarabi here with connotations wider than those of formal logic.

 2. Cf. above, sec. 33; Alfarabi, *Plato's "Laws,"* II (13:14–19, 15:7 ff.), *Political Regime*, pp. 55–57, *Virtuous City*, pp. 51–53.

 3. Cf. above, secs. 45 ff.

 4. Cf. Alfarabi, *Virtuous Religion*, fol. 53*r*.

 5. The causes or principles of the heavenly bodies. Alfarabi, *Political Regime*, pp. 2 ff., *Virtuous City*, pp. 19–20, 69.

 6. Alfarabi says "principles" and "principles." Cf. above, sec. 20.

 7. 19D, 21B–C, 29B ff. Cf. below, II, secs. 33, 35.

 8. Alfarabi elaborates this theme in the *Virtuous Religion*, fols. 58 ff., *Political Regime*, pp. 55:8–57:10. He presents two elaborate schemes based on it in his *Virtuous City* and *Political Regime*.

(56) 1. Cf. above, sec. 54.

 2. Above, secs. 23 ff.

 3. Alfarabi, *Virtuous Religion*, fols. 51*v*–52*v*.

 4. Cf. Aristotle *Nicomachean Ethics* x. 9. 1180ᵃ32–ᵇ23; Alfarabi, *Plato's "Laws,"* II (15:11 ff.).

 5. Above, secs. 23 ff.

 6. Apparently meaning "moral"; see above, secs. 35 ff., cf. sec. 41 n. 1.

(57) 1. Contrast Aristotle *Nicomachean Ethics* vi. 7. 1141ᵃ20 ff.

 2. Aristotle *Nicomachean Ethics* x. 7. 1177ᵃ33–ᵇ1. Alfarabi, *Virtuous City*, p. 57.

 3. "Practical" as distinguished from "incorporeal" and "natural." They are the intelligibles whose realization depends on deliberation, moral character, and art. Above, secs. 22 ff., 40.

 4. Alfarabi, *Plato's "Laws,"* II.

5. Consider Aristotle's objections in *Nicomachean Ethics* i. 6. 1096ᵇ35 ff.

6. Below, secs. 60 ff.

(58) 1. Below, II, sec. 8.

(59) 1. "Things" (*ashyāʾ*). The term *shayʾ* is used throughout in a variety of senses (roughly corresponding to "being"). It can signify particulars or universals (cf. above, sec. 1), what exists outside the mind or the intelligible ideas (as here), the objects of knowledge or of opinion and imagination (as in the rest of the section). Cf. below, III, secs. 4 n. 6, 19.

2. Cf. above, sec. 57 n. 3.

3. Cf. above, secs. 53 ff.; Alfarabi, *Virtuous Religion*, fol. 53*r*, *Virtuous City*, pp. 69–70 (note the possibility of *different* good or virtuous "religions," cf. *Political Regime*, p. 56).

(60) 1. ii. 375A ff., vi. 487B ff., *passim*. Cf. Alfarabi, *Virtuous City*, pp. 59–60.

2. Alfarabi, *Statesman*, sec. 93; above, sec. 33 n. 1.

(61) 1. *Republic* vi. 498B; cf. Aristotle *Meteorologica* ii. 2. 355ᵃ9 ff.

(62) 1. Sections 53, 57, 59.

2. Plato *Republic* vi. 489B.

3. Alfarabi, *Statesman*, sec. 29; Plato *Statesman* 259A–B.

(64) 1. Above, sec. 61 (46:6).

Part II: THE PHILOSOPHY OF PLATO

(2) 1. For details on the possible origins of the "explanations" of the dialogues' titles (many of which are marginal or inter-linear additions to the text of the unique manuscript), cf. F. Rosenthal and R. Walzer, *De Platonis Philosophia* (London, 1943), pp. xvi–xviii, 17 ff.

(3) 1. Read *kamāl lah* (A?) for *ghāyatih* in line 4.

(5) 1. Bracket *maʿnāh* in line 14 with A. The marginal note in A sets a small *ʿayn* above the first word which may suggest that it is to be read *ʿāmil* ("maker") rather than *ḥāmil* ("carrier").

2. Read *wa-yūjad* for *wa-yuʾkhadh* in line 7 with A.

3. Cf., also, Aristotle *Metaphysics* iv. 5–6.

(6) 1. Read <*wa-immā an yajhalah*> *wa-inn mā* for *wa-immā ann mā* in line 16. Cf. Alfarabi, *Logic*, fol. 79*r*:3.

(7) 1. The term used for "religion" in this section is *dīn* (cf. *millah*, above, I, secs. 33, 55 ff.). In the *Virtuous Religion* (fol. 52*v*:16–18), Alfarabi says *"millah* and *dīn* are almost synonyms." In Islam, "religious speculation" would refer to dialectical theology (*kalām*) and the "religious syllogistic art" to jurisprudence (*fiqh*). Cf. Alfarabi, *Enumeration of the*

Sciences, ch. 5. The "syllogistic art" (*al-ṣināᶜah al-qiyāsiyyah*) was, of course, employed by theologians as well.

(8)   1. Cf. Alfarabi, *Directive to the Path of Happiness* (*al-Tanbīh ᶜalā sabīl al-saᶜādah*) (Hyderabad, 1346 A.H.), pp. 25–26, *Logic,* fol. 4.
      2. Read *bi-jawāhir* in line 4 with A.
      3. Add *miqdār mā* after *kam* in line 7 with A.

(10) 1. Bracket <*min*> *dhālik* in line 5.

(11) 1. Add *mithl* after *faḥṣ* in line 7 with F.
      2. Read *wa-annah* for <*fa-tabayyan lah*> *annah* in line 14 with A.

(12) 1. Read *fuḥūṣ* for *ṣināᶜah* in line 3 with A.

(13) 1. Read *wa-inn* for *wa-lākin innamā* in line 2.
      2. Bracket *qaṣd al-muqtanīn lahā* in line 3.
      3. Throughout secs. 13–16, 20, the Arabic term is *fāḍil* ("virtuous").

(17) 1. Not *insān* (*anthrōpos,* "human being"), which is the usual term employed by Alfarabi, but "*male* human being" (*rajul, anēr*). The Arabic for "fortitude" in this section is *rajlah* ("manliness," the "male character").
      2. Cf. Rosenthal and Walzer, *op. cit.,* pp. xix, 9, 21.
      3. *Ibid.*

(18) 1. *Ibid.*

(20) 1. *Ibid.,* p. 21.

(21) 1. *Statesman?* Cf. Rosenthal and Walzer, *op. cit.,* pp. 21–22.

(22) 1. Cf. above, I, sec. 42 n. 2.
      2. Or "supplies, from the outset, the desired science and, from the outset, the desired way of life." There is a persistent ambiguity throughout this section as to whether there is one or two skills and faculties.
      3. Read *wa-ann kull wāḥidah minhumā* in line 10 with A (adopting *minhumā* for *baynahumā* in note).

(24) 1. *Lysis?* Cf. Rosenthal and Walzer, *op. cit.,* p. 22.

(25) 1. Read *yaltamisuhā* for *taltamisuhā*[2] in line 15 with A.

(26) 1. Plato *Phaedrus* 265D, 266B; cf. Alfarabi, *Harmonization of the Opinions of Plato and Aristotle,* pp. 2:12 ff., 8:20 ff.

(28) 1. Alfarabi, *Harmonization of the Opinions of Plato and Aristotle,* pp. 5:22–6:5.

(29) 1. Bracket *aw ᶜalā ... madīnah* in lines 17–18.
      2. Read *allatī* <*hiy ᶜalā al-ḥaqīqah fāḍilah*> in line 2.
      3. Cf. Rosenthal and Walzer, *op. cit.,* pp. 23–24.

(30) 1. *Ibid.,* pp. 24–25; cf. the beginning of sec. 30.
      2. Cf. Alfarabi, *Harmonization of the Opinions of Plato and Aristotle,* pp. 20–22, where he refers to the problem of the immortality of the soul.

3. Cf. Ibn ʿAqnīn's paraphrase of 18:3–19:13. A. S. Halkin, "Ibn ʿAḳnīn's Commentary on the Song of Songs," *Alexander Marx Jubilee Volume* (English Section; New York, 1950) p. 423 n. 152.

4. Cf. Aristotle *Historia Animalium* ii. 13. 505ᵃ28 ff.

5. Read *khilqatuhā* for *khilqatuh* in line 9 with Ibn ʿAqnīn.

6. Add *fīh* after *yakūn* in line 9 with Ibn ʿAqnīn.

7. Read *annah* for *ann* in line 10 with Ibn ʿAqnīn.

8. Read *wa-* for *aw* in line 4 with F and Ibn ʿAqnīn.

9. Read *wa-yabʿud* for *wa-baʿdā* in line 10 with Ibn ʿAqnīn.

10. Read *falidhālik* for *fabidhālik* in line 12 with Ibn ʿAqnīn.

11. Bracket *kayf yakūn* in line 15.

(32) 1. Read *al-muʿādi<ya>h* for *al-muḍāddah* in line 11 with A.

2. Cf. Alfarabi, *Harmonization of the Opinions of Plato and Aristotle*, p. 32:3–5, where he refers to the "story" of resurrection and judgment (*Republic* x). Above, I, secs. 40, 60.

(33) 1. Cf. Alfarabi, *Harmonization of the Opinions of Plato and Aristotle*, pp. 24–27, 30, where he classifies the *Timaeus* and the *Politeia* (*Republic*) among Plato's books "on divine things" (*fī al-rubūbiyyah*) and compares the statements contained in them with the "amazing" statements of the lawgivers and the learned men of various sects and religions. Above, I, secs. 40, 60.

2. Cf. above, I, sec. 55.

(34) 1. Read *al-siyar* for *al-sīrah* in line 1 with A.

(36) 1. Cf. Aristotle *Metaphysics* i. 6. 987ᵇ1–4, xiii. 4. 1078ᵇ17–21, xiii. 10. 1086ᵇ3–5.

2. Cf. Aristotle *Nicomachean Ethics* vi. 13, *Magna Moralia* i. 1. 1183ᵇ8–18, i. 9. 1187ᵃ5 ff., i. 34. 1198ᵃ10–21.

3. *Cleitophon?* Cf. Rosenthal and Walzer, *op. cit.*, pp. 27–28. Cf., also, Plato *Republic*, *Phaedrus* (above, sec. 27), and the distinction between the Socratic and the Platonic views of virtue in Aristotle *Magna Moralia* i. 1. 1182ᵃ15–29.

Part III: THE PHILOSOPHY OF ARISTOTLE

(1) 1. The expression *wa-akthar* ("and more") occurs also in Alfarabi's *Political Regime*, p. 70:10. Like *polus, pleistos, pleiōn,* and so on, it can mean "more," "for the most part," "very much," "much too much," but also "go beyond bounds," "have (or claim) too much," "do too many things" (cf. the way Alfarabi explains the difference between Aristotle and

Plato [*Harmonization of the Opinions of Plato and Aristotle*, p. 5:10–21] as the result of the "excess" of Aristotle's "natural power"), which again may be intended as praise or blame. This ambiguity characterizes Alfarabi's account of Aristotle's philosophy as a whole.

2. Although Alfarabi does not mention any of Aristotle's "early" works, the themes of many of these works are present in the following account of the "position from which Aristotle started." Following the classical tradition, Alfarabi calls these works Aristotle's "public" or "civic" works on "external philosophy." (Alfarabi, *Introduction to Aristotle* [*Fīmā yanbaghī an yuqaddam qabl taʿallum al-falsafah*] in *Alfārābī's philosophische Abhandlungen*, ed. Fr. Dieterici [Leiden, 1890], p. 50:16 ff., *Logic*, fol. 91v; above, I, sec. 55.) Accordingly, Aristotle's "beginning" should perhaps be understood to mean his "public," "civic," or "dialectical" arguments on the "perfection of man." This would explain why Alfarabi draws upon the "early" works as well as upon the "dialectical" parts of "later" works, e.g., *Nicomachean Ethics, De Anima*, and *Metaphysics*. The guiding principle is thus not the date of composition. What is being explained is not a "development," and certainly not a "gradual development" away from Plato, but the kind of argument used. Cf. above, II, secs. 27, 36, below, secs. 15–16.

3. Cf. above, II, sec. 1.

4. I.e., over and above the "merely necessary" soundness of each. Below, sec. 2 (60:20–21, 64:18–65:9).

(2) 1. Above, II, sec. 18.

2. Above, II, sec. 37.

3. Below, secs. 3 (63, 69:8 ff.), 4, 91 ff.

4. Read *fīmā yudrik bi-al-ḥiss lā fīmā* in lines 9–10. Cf. Aristotle *Metaphysics* i. 1. 980ᵃ21–ᵇ25.

5. Above, II, sec. 9.

(3) 1. Or "problems" (*maṭlūbāt*). Even when discussing Aristotle's logical works (below, secs. 5 ff.) Alfarabi uses this term alone where the Arabic translations of these works distinguish between *maṭlūbāt* ("problems") and *masāʾil* ("questions"). Cf. Alfarabi, *Logic*, fol. 30v:12–14.

2. Above, I, sec. 2.

3. Above, I, secs. 20, 34, II, secs. 13–16.

4. Or "accidents" (*aʿrāḍ*).

5. Above, I, sec. 6.

6. *Ibid.*

7. Above, I, secs. 23 ff.

8. Above, I, sec. 20.

(4) 1. Cf., however, below, sec. 13 (81:8 ff.) and n. 2.
     2. Above, sec. 3 (69:17).
     3. Above, I, secs. 23–24.
     4. Above, secs. 3 (70:15 ff.)–4 (71:5 ff.).
     5. Aristotle *Metaphysics* iii. 6.
     6. "Things" (*ashyā*). Cf. above, I, sec. 59 n. 1.
(6) 1. "Matters" (*umūr*).
     2. Throughout this section: "things" (*ashyā*) or "matters"
        (*umūr*). Cf. the use of "rules" (*qawānīn*), below, secs. 13, 14.
(7) 1. Above, I, secs. 5–6.
     2. Above, I, secs. 5, 8.
     3. Above, I, secs. 6–7, 11–20.
     4. "Angel" (*malak* F) or "king" (*malik*).
     5. The formula of the text corresponds to $A:B::C:D$.
     6. Cf. above, I, sec. 53.
(9) 1. Above, I, sec. 53.
(12) 1. Above, I, secs. 40 ff., 46, 50 ff., 55.
(13) 1. Aristotle *Topics* viii. 5, *De Sophisticis Elenchis* chs. 11, 34.
     2. Cf. Aristotle *De Sophisticis Elenchis* ch. 3; above, sec. 4
        (71:14). In his paraphase of *De Sophisticis Elenchis* (*Logic*,
        fol. 52*v*) Alfarabi divides fallacies into those that take the
        form of "reasoning" or "syllogism" (*qiyās*) and those that do
        not. The latter are "the human states, the aptitudes, and the
        states of character that turn man away from truth to error:
        for instance, love or hatred for an opinion. . . . These are
        more appropriately dealt with in the *Rhetoric* and the *Poetics*."
        This is the class to which "silencing" belongs. Cf. Aristotle
        De Sophisticis Elenchis chs. 5. 167ᵇ8 ff., 15. 174ᵇ19 ff.
     3. Aristotle *De Sophisticis Elenchis* ch. 12. 172ᵇ10–28 ("fal-
        lacy").
     4. As in a number of other terms in this section, Alfarabi does
        not use the Arabic terms used in the Arabic translations of
        Aristotle's *De Sophisticis Elenchis*. The term rendered "flat-
        tery" is *dahn*, which means also "to weaken" ("weakness of
        opinion" is found among the Arabic renderings of "paradox").
        Both "flattery" and "weakening" are implied in Aristotle's
        description of the way to entrap someone into a paradox,
        De Sophisticis Elenchis ch. 12. 172ᵇ36 ff.
(15) 1. Add F; cf. above, sec. 12.
     2. Aristotle *Rhetoric*. Cf. Alfarabi, *Logic*, fols. 112*r* ff.; above,
        I, secs. 44 ff., II, sec. 36.
(16) 1. Aristotle *Poetics*. Cf. Alfarabi, *Logic*, fols. 122*r*–23*r;* above,
        I, sec. 55, II, sec. 9.
     2. Above, sec. 4.

(18) 1. Aristotle *Physics* ii. 1. 193ᵃ30–31, *Metaphysics* v. 8. 1017ᵇ25.
"Whatness" or "quiddity" (*māhiyyah*) is derived from the
particle *mā* and the pronoun *huw* ("what it [*or* this] is") and
indicates the differentiae of the specific substance, its shape or
form (*eidos* or *morphē*). It is frequently used synonymously
with "form" (*ṣūrah*) (cf. above, I, sec. 6, below, secs. 22
[93:2], 25 [94:12–14]) and "essence" (*dhāt*) (cf. below,
sec. 54 n. 2).

(22) 1. Cf. Aristotle *Physics* ii. 3. 194ᵇ26, 195ᵃ20.

(39) 1. E.g., Empedocles, Anaxagoras, and Leucippus; cf. Aristotle
De Generatione et Corruptione i. 1–2.

(44) 1. I.e., *Fire, Air, Water,* and *Earth.* Aristotle *De Generatione
et Corruptione* ii. 3. 330ᵇ2–4; below, sec. 59.
      2. Above, secs. 36 ff.; Aristotle *De Caelo* iii. 7. 305ᵇ20 ff.
      3. I.e., the elementary qualities (hot, cold, dry, moist) diversely
coupled so as to constitute the "simple" bodies. Aristotle *De
Generatione et Corruptione* ii. 1–3; below, sec. 54 (104:1–2).

(54) 1. Although the previous section refers to the final chapter of
De Generatione et Corruptione, secs. 54–63 (which do not
discuss the particular phenomena treated in *Meteorologica*
i–iii) continue to speak of subjects treated in this work.
      2. "Whatness" (*māhiyyah*) throughout the remaining sections.
The term *dhāt,* which is normally rendered "essence," does
not occur in the remaining sections except in secs. 82
(118:17), 90 (123:10), 92 (124:17, 125:2).
      3. Cf. Aristotle *De Caelo* iv, *De Generatione et Corruptione* ii.
4–5, *Meteorologica* i. 3.

(59) 1. Read *al-nār* for *al-lahīb* in line 15. Cf. below, sec. 60 (107:5);
Aristotle *De Generatione et Corruptione* ii. 4. 331ᵇ24.

(63) 1. Above, sec. 54 n. 1.

(66) 1. Read *hawāᵓ wa-māᵓ* for *qiwā* in line 7. Aristotle *De Anima*
ii. 8. 419ᵇ18 ff., ii. 9. 421ᵇ9 ff.

(68) 1. This work formed an appendix to Aristotle's *Meteorologica.*

(71) 1. Sections 69–71. (pseudo-)Aristotle *De Plantis.*

(74) 1. Sections 72–74. Aristotle "De Naturis Animalium" (*De Parti-
bus Animalium, De Generatione Animalium,* and *Historia
Animalium*).

(78) 1. Section 75–78. Aristotle *De Anima* i. Cf. below, sec. 95.
      2. *De Sanitate et Morbo.*

(81) 1. Aristotle *De Longitudine et Brevitate Vitae.*

(82) 1. Aristotle *De Vita et Morte.*

(85) 1. Aristotle *De Incessu Animalium.*

(86) 1. Aristotle *De Respiratione.*

(87) 1. Aristotle *De Somno et Vigilia.*
      2. Aristotle *De Somniis.*

3. Aristotle *De Divinatione per Somnum.*

4. Below, sec. 95.

(88) 1. Aristotle *De Memoria et Reminiscentia.*

2. Aristotle *De Anima* ii.

(89) 1. The transition appears to refer to Aristotle *De Anima* ii–iii.

(90) 1. Cf. Alfarabi, *Intellect*, secs. 13 ff.

(91) 1. Above, I, sec. 18.

2. Above, secs. 2 (60:17–61:2), 3 (63, 69:8 ff.), 4; cf. I, secs. 21 ff.

3. Above, I, secs. 23 ff.

(95) 1. Above, secs. 78, 87, 90.

(96) 1. Above, secs. 63, 74, 76, 78, 90.

(97) 1. Read *ʿamaliyyah* for *ʿaqliyyah* in line 11.

(98) 1. Above, sec. 97.

(99) 1. Above, secs. 31–35, 38, 49.

2. Above, sec. 97.

3. Above, I, sec. 13 n. 2.

4. This apparently refers to the faculties stated above, secs. 87–89.

5. Above, sec. 91.

6. Above, I, secs. 16 ff.

7. Above, I, secs. 18 ff.

8. Cf. Alfarabi, *Aristotle's "Metaphysics,"* pp. 34–38.

9. For *al-ʿaql* in line 13 read *al-fiʿl* (A) and add *al-madanī* with al-Baghdādī.

10. For *al-ʿaql* in line 14 read *al-fiʿl* (A?).

Notes to the Arabic Text of
The Attainment of Happiness

The numbers on the margin of the translated text refer to the pages and lines of the first and so far the only editions of the three parts of the Arabic text, which have appeared separately as follows:

I. *The Attainment of Happiness* (*Taḥṣīl al-saᶜādah*) (Hyderabad, 1345 A.H.).

II. *The Philosophy of Plato* (*Falsafat Aflāṭun*), ed. Franz Rosenthal and Richard Walzer (London, 1943).

III. *The Philosophy of Aristotle* (*Falsafat Arisṭūṭālīs*), ed. Muhsin Mahdi (Beirut, 1961).

The edited text of Parts II and III is based on a unique Arabic manuscript (A) preserved in the Aya Sofya Library in Constantinople (No. 4833, fols. 1*v*–9*v* and 19*v*–59*r*, respectively) and Falaquera's Hebrew paraphrase (F) contained in *Reschith Chokmah*, ed. M. David (Berlin, 1902), pp. 72–78 and 78–92, respectively. (There exists a manuscript copy of a Latin translation of Falaquera's work in the Bibliothèque Nationale, Paris, Départment des Manuscrits, Latin, No. 6991*A*. It is, however, practically useless for establishing Falaquera's text apart from pointing out certain obvious mistakes in David's edition.) After the publication of the text of Part II, A. S. Halkin published the text of Ibn ᶜAqnīn's paraphrase of a part of II, sec. 30. The well-known disciple of Maimonides quotes this passage in his *Commentary on the Song of Songs*. (Above, II, sec. 30 n. 3.) The notes to Parts II and III indicate such cases where readings other than those of the edited text were adopted and supply their authority. Where the readings differ from what is reported in the text or *apparatus criticus* of Part II, they are based on a fresh examination of the Aya Sofya manuscript and Falaquera's Hebrew paraphrase.

This procedure did not prove practical in respect to Part I. The Hyderabad text (H) is not an edition but a printer's copy. It is ostensibly based on "two manuscripts" (p. 37 n. 1). These are not identified, however. Such indications as can be gathered from other treatises by Alfarabi printed in Hyderabad at about the same time (cf., e.g., *Sharḥ risālat Zaynūn al-kabīr al-Yūnānī* [Hyderabad, 1349 A.H.], p. 2, *Masāᵓil mutafarriqah* [Hyderabad, 1344 A.H.], p. 24) point to the two "almost identical" manuscript collections preserved in the State Library of Rampur and numbered *Ḥikmat* 150 (said to be in "ancient script") and 151 (said to be younger and dated 1276 A.H.). The catalogue of that library (*Fihriste kutube ᶜArabī* [Rampur, 1902], p. 400, cf. p. 403) confirms this information in part, and adds that the two collections are made up of 392 and 410 pages, and the *Attainment of Happiness* of 50 and 62 pages, respectively. It is not possible in the absence of a published catalogue to ascertain whethei or not the manuscript No. 149 preserved in the library of Nadwat al-ʿUlamāʾ in Lucknow was utilized in the Hyderabad text (as may be suggested by the symbol N which designates this manuscript in *Sharḥ risālat Zyanūn*), or whether this manuscript contains the *Attainment of Happiness*. In any event, the practical identity of the two manuscripts utilized is attested by the lack of variants (the one exception is the variant reported on p. 46 n. 1) in the Hyderabad text. None of these manuscripts is at present easily accessible.

In order to establish a more reliable basis for the present translation, the Hyderabad text has been collated with Falaquera's Hebrew paraphrase and with two manuscript copies of the Arabic original. The first (BM) is the manuscript preserved in the British Museum, London (Add. 7518 *Rich.*, fols. 88*v*–110*v*), copied in Isfahan in 1105 A.H. The second (EH) is the manuscript preserved in the Topkapu Saray Library, Constantinople (Emanet Hazinesi, No. 1730, fols. 52*r*–62*v*), dated 1089 A.H. Of the two manuscripts, EH is closer to the Hyderabad text, but all three (H, BM, and EH) form a close family. In general, the readings of the manuscripts were preferred to those of the printed text. Falaquera's Hebrew paraphrase (F), contained in *Reschith Chokmah*, pp. 61–72, is, of course, based on a copy older than all the extant Arabic manuscripts. That copy must have belonged to a different family representing a more complete text. The readings from Falaquera have been translated back to Arabic and are given here in quotation marks.

The following notes are drawn from the material being gathered with a view to an eventual edition of the Arabic text of the *Attainment of Happiness*. They are not conceived as an *apparatus criticus* to the Hyderabad text. They simply list the readings adopted for the purpose of the present translation and indicate their authority. The numbers refer to the pages and lines of the Hyderabad text. They are followed by the reading of the printed text and then by the reading adopted here and its authority. In all cases where the reference is unmistakable, the reading of the Hyderabad text is not reproduced and the note simply records the adopted reading:

H = Alfarabi, *Taḥṣīl al-saʿādah* (Hyderabad, 1345 A.H.)

BM = Alfarabi, *Taḥṣīl al-saʿādah*, MS, British Museum (London), Add. 7518 *Rich.*

EH = Alfarabi, *Taḥṣīl al-saʿādah*, MS, Topkapu Saray Library (Constantinople), Emanet Hazinesi, No. 1730.

F = Falaquera, *Reschith Chokmah*, ed. M. David (Berlin, 1902).

St. = Alfarabi, *Aphorisms of the Statesman*, ed. D. M. Dunlop (Cambridge, 1961).

2 4 *al-ākhirah* BM, EH, F ‖ 6 *mutayaqqanā bihā* BM?, EH, F
3 8 *al-muthbitah:* + *lah* BM, F ‖ 10 *yūqiʿunā: yūqiʿ lanā* BM, EH ‖

11 *tūqiʿunā: tūqiʿ lanā* BM, EH ‖ 13 *nastaʿmil: "nasluk"* F ‖ *ilā:*
+ *"al-yaqīn wa-nasluk fī maṭlūb ākhar ṭarīqā naṣīr minh ilā mā
huw mithāluh aw khayāluh aw ṭarīqā yufḍī binā ilā"* F ‖ 19 *takhuṣṣ
wāḥidah* BM

4 1 *bi-ṣināʿah* BM, EH ‖ 6 *fa-tuḍallil* BM, EH ‖ *wa-yataḥayyar: aw
tuḥayyirah fīh* BM, EH ‖ 15 *bimā: bihā mā* ‖ 16 *fīh: fīhā* BM,
EH, F ‖ 19 *aw li-kathīr* BM, EH

5 2 *wa-:* + *"idhā kānat al-maʿlūmāt al-uwal fī jins min al-ajnās hiy
bi-aʿyānihā asbāb mā yashtamil ʿalayh dhālik al-jins"* F ‖ 5 *idhā[1]:
idh* EH, F ‖ 19 *bi-wujūd* BM, F

6 1 (transfer this line to the top of p. 7) ‖ 2 *[ʿalayh]* BM, F ‖ 5
ʿalā: + *mā huw* BM ‖ 10 *lā yatakhaṭṭ<ā>* BM ‖ 11 *fᴂidhā* BM, EH

7 5 *[min]* BM, EH ‖ 9 *maʿlūmah* BM, EH ‖ 10 *majhūlah* BM, EH ‖
11 *-hā: bihā* BM ‖ 19 *fa-natakhaṭṭā* BM?, EH?

8 3 *wujūd mabdᴂih* BM, EH ‖ 11 *wa-huw* BM, EH, F ‖ 13 *bi-al-
aʿdād: al-aʿdād*

9 1 *wa-lākin: dhālik* BM, EH ‖ 2 *wa-kān: kān* BM, EH ‖ 3 *[min[2]]*
BM, EH ‖ 4 *famā* BM, EH ‖ 13 *al-taʿlīm* ‖ 14 *alladhī:* + *<fīh>*
‖ 15 *yanẓur:* + *fīh* BM, EH ‖ 17 *fa-yakuff* EH ‖ *idh* BM, EH

10 3 *al-ʿaql* BM, EH ‖ 5 *ukhidhā* BM, EH ‖ 6 *wa-lam: lam* BM, EH
‖ 9 *allatī hiy: "thumm ilā"* F, St. (165:10 n.) ‖ *wa-ilā al-athqāl*
BM, EH, St. (165:11) ‖ 10 *ayḍā: aṣlā* BM, EH, F ‖ *thumm:* +
ilā EH ‖ 11 *wa-taṣawwurih:* + *wa-fī an yuʿqal* BM ‖ 14 *[muḥtājā
fī an yaṣīr]* ‖ 18 *mutākhimā* BM, EH, St. (165:16 n.) ‖ *al-jins*
BM, EH, St. (165:16)

11 14 *wa-mādhā* BM, EH

12 2 *al-wujūd* BM, EH ‖ 4 *mabādiʾ* BM ‖ 6 *yaʾtī* BM ‖ 7 *fa-ḥaṣalat*
BM, EH ‖ 9 *istaʿmalnā* BM, EH

13 2 *yaḍṭarruh* BM, EH ‖ 3 *aw: wa-* EH, F ‖ *wa-yartaqī* BM, EH ‖
5 *[al-naẓar]* F ‖ 7 *mabādiʾ:* + *ukhar laysat bi-ajsām wa-lā fī ajsām
wa-lā kānat wa-lā yakūn* (read *takūn*) *fī ajsām yakūn qad intahā
bi-al-naẓar fī al-ḥayawān al-nāṭiq ilā shabīh mā intahā ilayh ʿind
naẓarih fī al-ajsām al-samᴂiyyah fa-yaṣīr ilā an yaṭṭaliʿ ʿalā mabādiʾ
EH ‖ 9 ʿalayhā:* + *ʿind* BM, EH ‖ 12 *al-taʿlīm: "al-ʿālam"* F, St.
(166:12) ‖ 18 *bimā: innamā* BM, EH

14 3 *lah: "yaḥṣul bih"* F ‖ 5 *[lā]* EH, F ‖ 8 *yablughuh* BM, EH, F

15 1 *bimā: mimmā* BM, EH ‖ 9 *"wujūduhā"* F, St. (166:19) ‖ *ʿalayhā*
St. (166:19), F ‖ 12 *al-wujūd:* + *"wa-huw aqrabuhā ilayh ḥattā
yantahī ilā ākhirihā rutbah fī al-wujūd"* F ‖ *abʿaduhā* BM, EH, F
‖ 14 *lah: al-ilāh* BM, EH, F ‖ 15 *wa-lā fī* BM, EH, F ‖ 19 *"tanfaʿ
fī bulūghih"* F

16 3 *[wa-li-ajl mādhā]* ‖ 11 *al-wujūd kadhālik* BM, EH ‖ 11–12 *fī
jumlah mā: fīmā* BM ‖ 12 *ukhar* BM ‖ 14 *yantahī:* + *ilā* BM, EH

17 2[1,2] *uʿṭiyat* BM, EH ‖ 3 *uʿṭiyat* BM, EH ‖ 5 *ʿaqal kayf* BM, EH ‖

8 *istinād:* ījād BM, EH ‖ 11 *tadūm* BM ‖ 12 *tadūm:* + <*wāḥidah bi-al-ʿadad bal tadūm*> ‖ 14 *taqtarin*[1]*: tuqran* BM

18 1 *aqṣā: aydā* ‖ *bi-al-irādah* BM, EH ‖ 8 *tarkībāt* BM, EH ‖ *ṣuwariyyah* BM ‖ 13 *māʿalayh: fāʿiliyyah* BM ‖ 16 *mukhālifah* (cf. 19:3)

19 2 *allatī:* + *yūjad limā* EH ‖ 7 *lahā:* + *ʿindamā yūjad* BM, EH ‖ 14 [*wa-*] EH ‖ 17 *hādhā:* + *an* BM, EH ‖ 19 *yanfaʿuhum: bi-baʿḍihim* BM

20 5 [*lā*] EH ‖ *māhiyyah: mihnah* EH ‖ 7 *zamān:* + *mā* BM, EH ‖ 8 *fa-al-mihnah* EH ‖ 13 *wa-al-mustanbiṭ* BM, EH, F ‖ 16 *anfaʿ*

21 5 *allatī:* + *"bihā"* F ‖ 6 *bimā: "mā"* F ‖ 7 *ghāyah:* + *mā* BM, EH ‖ 16 *tabtadī: "tatabaddal"* F ‖ *lā: innamā* BM, EH ‖ 17 *illā maʿ: al-anfaʿ* BM, EH ‖ *aw*[3]*: idhā* BM

22 5 *al-uwal: "al-ūlā"* F ‖ 12, 13 *gharaḍ* BM ‖ 12 *ṣināʿah:* + *ṣināʿah* EH ‖ 14 *al-ḥiraf: al-siyar* BM, EH ‖ 19 *wa-li-ajl* BM, EH

23 2 [*wa-*] ‖ 3 *annah: in* BM ‖ 4 *khayyir:* + *illā* (read *lā*) *khayyir* BM, EH ‖ 7 *khulquh* BM, EH ‖ *fikrih* BM, EH ‖ <*wa-*>ʿalā ‖ 11 *wa-kadhālik* BM, EH ‖ 13 *fa-faḍīlatuh* BM ‖ *wa-kull* BM ‖ *fī: min* BM, EH ‖ 17 [*minhā*] ‖ 18 [*lammā kānat*] ‖ 19 *al-muqtarinah* BM

24 2 *wa-bayān: faʾinn* ‖ 7 *gharaḍ* BM ‖ *bi-manzil* BM ‖ 16 *lah: tilk* ‖ [*wa-*] BM, EH ‖ *faḍīlatuh* BM, EH

25 6 *kadhalik:* + <*ṣāḥib*> ‖ 9 *wa-tilk* BM, EH ‖ 12 *natamakkan* BM ‖ 14 *al-ṣināʿah: al-ṣināʿāt* BM, EH ‖ 18 *al-juzʾiyyah: al-ḥarbiyyah* EH? ‖ 19 *al-ṣanāʾiʿ:* + *al-ḥarbiyyah* EH?

26 13 *faʾin:* + *kān* BM, EH ‖ 16 *an*[2]*:* + <*yakūn*>

27 5 *allatī*[1]*: "innamā"* F ‖ *munfaridah* BM?, F ‖ 6 *al-khulqiyyah: "al-fikriyyah"* F ‖ 8 *huw: hawā* EH, F ‖ 9 *huw bih: "hawāh"* F, EH? ‖ 13 *illā an: "allā"* F ‖ 18 *al-faḍīlah al-fikriyyah hiy: "faḍīlah khulqiyyah ghayr"* F ‖ 19 *al-faḍīlah:* + *"al-fikriyyah"* F ‖ *al-khayriyyah: al-khayr* BM, EH

28 2 *tastanbiṭuhā: "tustanbaṭ bihā"* F ‖ 8 *al-thaʿlab* BM, EH, F ‖ 12 *in lam yuqsar* EH ‖ 19 *tashbah* BM, EH, F

29 2 *lays:* + *innamā* BM, EH ‖ 5, 13, 15 *al-ʿamaliyyah* BM, EH, F ‖ 10 *hādhih:* + *"fī"* F ‖ 19 *wa-taʿlīm* EH ‖ *ʿadīdah: wāḥidah* BM, EH

30 3 *wa-yuʾkhadhū* BM ‖ 8 *fī:* + *marātib* EH ‖ *riʾāsah:* + *riʾāsah* BM, EH

31 6 *al-malakāt:* + <*min*> ‖ 7 *al-manṭiqiyyah* BM, EH ‖ 10 *ʿalā talaqqī: ḥattā yulaqqin* EH ‖ 11 *ṣināʿatuh* BM, EH ‖ 12 [*faḍāʾil*] BM ‖ 16 *ʿalayh al-ān: al-amr ʿalayh* BM, EH ‖ *al-manāzil* BM, EH

32 2 *māhiyyah: mihnah* BM?, EH, F ‖ 9 *min al-māhiyyah al-juzʾiyyah: "hiy al-mihnah* (= BM, EH) *al-ḥarbiyyah"* F ‖ 14 *li-insān:* + *insān* BM, EH ‖ 15 *al-juzʾī: "al-ḥarbī"* F ‖ 16 *al-juzʾī: al-ḥarbī* BM, F ‖ 16, 17 *al-juzʾiyyah: al-ḥarbiyyah* BM ‖ 19 *al-manṭiqiyyah* BM ‖ *al-ʿulūm: al-umūr* BM, EH

33 4 *lam: thumm* ‖ *yaj·al* BM, EH ‖ 5 *al-mithālāt:* + *mithālāt* EH ‖
tukhayyil BM, EH ‖ 6 *al-taṣdīq: al-taqrīr* BM ‖ [*bih*] BM ‖ 7
bi-ṭuruq BM ‖ 9 *ishturiṭat* BM, EH ‖ 10 *mashhūrah: mashwariyyah*
BM, EH ‖ 11 *lahā: bihā* BM, EH ‖ 12 *talīn: tariqq* EH ‖ 13
lahā²: bihā BM ‖ [*bih*] EH ‖ *wa-taqsū* BM, EH ‖ *takhbū: ta·āf* (cf.
33:17)

34 1 *al-ṣinfayn* BM, EH ‖ 6 *al-·ulūm* BM, EH ‖ 8–9 [*yunāqiḍuh*
wa-muḍāddat mā yu-] BM, EH (cf. 35:14) ‖ 11 *wuṭṭiʾat* BM, EH?
‖ 12<*a*>*w aktharihim* ‖ 14 *fī: fa-yumayyiz* BM, EH ‖ 15 *wa-yuḥṣī*
‖ 16 *·adad* BM, EH

35 9 [*aw¹*] EH ‖ 10 [*wa-¹*] BM, EH ‖ 13 *al-khayr: al-jins* BM, EH
‖ 18 *ḥarbiyyah* ‖ 19 *yantafi·ūn* BM

36 1, 3, 5 *mihnah* BM, EH ‖ 3 *al-ḥarbiyyah* ‖ *yufawwaḍ* BM ‖ 10
qarībā: fa-ra·īsā ‖ *fa-māddatuhumā: fa-khādimā* BM?, EH ‖
faḍīlatih, BM, EH ‖ 11 *aw fī:* + *kull* BM, EH

37 9 *tarsakh* EH? ‖ 11 *li-riʾāsah* BM, EH ‖ *wa-lidhālik* EH ‖ 12 *ḥāluh:*
+ *ḥāl* BM, EH ‖ 13 [*nafsah*] BM ‖ *khāṣṣiyyā:* + *madaniyyā* BM ‖
14 *ṣinā·atuh:* + *ṣinā·ah* BM, EH ‖ 18 *mā ista·hal* BM ‖ 18–19 *bi-*
malakatih wa-bi-mihnatih BM, EH

38 1 *al-ghāyah* BM, EH ‖ 7 *al-takhyīlāt* BM ‖ 11 <*wa-*>*al-muntaza·*
‖ 12 *li-yakmul* BM, F ‖ 14 *·alā mā: kamā* BM, EH ‖ 19 *malakatah*
BM, EH

39 1 [*bihā*] BM, EH, F ‖ 3, 4¹,² *tasta·mil* BM, EH ‖ 6 *bashariyyah:*
bisharīṭah BM, EH ‖ 10 *ghayrih* BM, EH, F ‖ 11 *an: "man"* F ‖
12 *man siwāh* BM, EH, F ‖ 14 *mā²: man* BM, EH ‖ *hal huw an:*
huw alladhī

40 11 *millah* BM, EH ‖ 12 *al-millah* ‖ 13 *al-barrāniyyah* BM, EH ‖
fa-al-millah EH ‖ 18¹,² *al-millah* BM, EH

41 6 *wa-al-·adam* BM, EH ‖ 10 *al-kāʾinah: al-makāniyyah* BM, EH ‖
yataḥarrā BM, EH ‖ 15 *yumkin* BM, EH

42 1 *yusaddid bihā* BM, EH ‖ 2 *mihnah* BM, EH ‖ 4 *nawāmīs* BM,
EH ‖ *mihnatah mihnah* BM, EH ‖ 6 *mā: man* BM, EH, F ‖ 9
[*allatī*] F ‖ 10 *mā: "man"* F ‖ 12 *fīh: minh* BM, EH + *awwalā*
BM, EH, F

43 2 *rubbamā: wa-bimā* EH ‖ 2–3 *ṣinā·atuh wa-mihnatuh wa-faḍīlatuh*
BM, EH, F ‖ 5 *idh* BM, EH, F ‖ 8 *wa-huw: huw* BM, EH, F ‖
10 *bi-jamī·* BM ‖ 15 *aw: idh* BM ‖ *bi-jamī·* ‖ 17 <*wa-*>*dūn* ‖ 19
[*kulluh*] BM

44 7, 12¹,² *millah* ‖ 8 *tabayyan:* + *min* ‖ *bi-baṣīrah* BM, EH ‖ 9
bi-takhayyul EH ‖ 11 [*fī nafsih¹*] ‖ 12 *lah¹:* + <*bal*> ‖ *mutakhay-*
yal BM ‖ *baqā: wa-yaqīn* BM, EH ‖ 15 *al-·ulūm:* + *al-naẓarriyyah*
EH ‖ *muwaṭṭaʾā* BM

45 14 *yazūr: yuzid* EH ‖ 17 *ta·allam* BM, F

46 1 *fīhā* BM, EH ‖ 3 *yaqharān* BM, EH ‖ 7 *ajzāʾ min: juzʾ min* *azjā* BM, F || 9 *ʿalayhā* BM, EH || 15 *aw al-imām huw bi-mihnatih wa-bi-ṣināʿatih* BM, EH || 17 *bi-mihnatih* BM, F || *marḍā:* +*lah* BM || 18 *al-ālāt* BM + *allatī* BM (cf., however, St. 124:1 and 3) || 19 *ṭibbah* BM, EH, F || [*an*] F?, cf. St. (124:5) || *yakūn:* + *lah* BM, EH

47 1 [*an*] || 5 *wa-al-ṭuruq* BM.

INDEX

[Names and titles cited by Alfarabi]